Best of
Books By the Bed #3

**What Writers Are Reading
Before Lights Out**

Edited by Cheryl Olsen and Eric Olsen

BRIGHTCITY**BOOKS**
brightcitybooks.com

Copyright © 2015 by Cheryl Olsen and Eric Olsen

All Rights Reserved. No part of this book may be reproduced in any manner without the express written consent of the publisher, except in the case of brief excerpts in critical reviews or articles. Inquiries should be addressed to info@wewantedtobewriters.com.

ISBN: 978-0-9795898-0-5

Edited by Cheryl Olsen and Eric Olsen
Cover photo by Eric Olsen, cover design by Bill Girsch
Cover cat: Tyson
Cover painting: "Le Reve" ("The Dream") by Pablo Picasso (1932)

Thanks!

Writers write; readers read. When the former do the latter, we all win. At a time when an estimated 5000 books are published every day, it's nice to have some folks who know their way between the end flaps sharing their insights and helping the rest of us make informed choices about what to read next.

We are enormously indebted to the contributors herein, as well as to writers everywhere whose love of language and words and their purposeful arrangement on the page enrich all our lives. This book (and its two predecessors) is an expression of gratitude and admiration for their talents and generosity.

Table of Contents

- 1   Introduction
- 4   Dale Bridges
- 6   David Corbett
- 10   Lucille Lang Day
- 14   Polly Dugan
- 18   Grant Faulkner
- 22   Wendy Fox
- 25   Clifford Garstang
- 28   Kathie Giorgio
- 32   Kathy Girsch
- 35   Kate Gray
- 38   Stefanie Paige Gunning
- 42   Therése Halscheid
- 46   Tara Ison
- 48   Pam Jenoff
- 50   Nicole C. Kear
- 54   Kim Korson
- 57   April Linder
- 61   Jonnie Martin
- 65   Ilana Masad
- 68   Felicia Mitchell
- 71   Mary Morris

73	Valerie Nieman
77	Cheryl Olsen
81	Eric Olsen
86	Judy Reeves
89	Kathryn Leigh Scott
91	Nancy Slavin
95	Therese Walsh
97	Books By Our Contributors
103	Fiction Discussed By Our Contributors
115	Poetry Discussed By Our Contributors
117	Nonfiction Discussed By Our Contributors
123	About the Editors

Introduction

by Eric Olsen

A common theme runs through the 28 contributions in this third volume of our *Best of Books by the Bed* collection, and that theme is *mess*. Besides discussing the books they're currently reading at night before dropping off to sleep, or books they're planning to read next, or books they have read but haven't quite gotten around to putting away, a rather intriguing number of our contributors also talk about the mess of books by their beds, starting with Dale Bridges and his "tome towers," "disjointed Jenga-like constructions that appear stable but crash to the floor if you look at them funny."

Now I can't look—whether funny or any other way—at the stacks of books by my own bed, at that *mess*, without thinking "tome towers," and thank you very much, Dale, for that image ….

Mary Morris tells us about a Japanese word she recently discovered that perhaps most typifies her particular affliction when it comes to books: *Tsundoku*. It roughly translates to "someone who buys books and lets them pile up without reading them." Mary writes, "I suffer somewhat from this trait. I buy books because I just must have them and then they sit around, sometimes for years, before I actually read them. The books at my bedside flow over to the dresser and then out into several piles stacked in the hall."

I'm likewise afflicted, and I must say it's nice to finally have a name for the affliction, not that having a name for it moderates in any way my impulse to buy books I may never get around to reading. But it is good to have interesting books around, I believe, books I intend to read at some point, such intention somehow giving shape and substance to an otherwise vague future. And I can't shake the feeling that something in books stacked nearby, especially good books, seeps out while we sleep, and may have a beneficial impact on one's own writing, and no matter what a mess the books might be.

But then I guess that's why so many writers seem to have messes of books by the bed. As Grant Faulkner (no relation to William, he insists) writes while discussing how "messy and sprawling" his own reading life has become, "I don't think 'messy' and 'sprawling' have to carry negative connotations, though."

Indeed not. In fact, mess is our friend. This is hardly a new notion, of course. Einstein, no slouch when it came to having lots of new ideas, had a notoriously sloppy office, and maintained that the mess helped him think. And I'm reminded of Edgar Wind's 1960 essay, *Art and Anarchy*, in which he argues that "a certain amount of turmoil and confusion is likely to call forth creative energies. As we know from the uneasy lives that were led by Dante, Michelangelo or Spenser (not to speak of Mozart or of Keats), the outward circumstances under which great art is produced are often far from reassuring."

Of course, by "turmoil" or "confusion," Wind is talking about such things as war, famine, revolution, pestilence, as well as drug and alcohol addictions and tumultuous and illicit affairs, complete with angry cuckolded husbands waving swords, not an unsteady tome tower by a bed. But the differences might be more of degree than substance. Numerous studies show a clear relationship between a person's tendency toward and tolerance of mess and that individual's creative abilities.

So bottom line? Put more books on that tome tower, and sweet dreams!

About the cover:

The cat on the cover is Tyson, a rescue kitty from New York City, now residing in California. He misses New York, though not the rats that were bigger than he is. He especially enjoys sitting by copies of *The New Yorker* and *The New York Review of Books*.

The painting on the wall above Tyson is a print of "Le Reve" ("The Dream") by Pablo Picasso. Supposedly he painted it in one afternoon in 1932. The woman in the painting is apparently his 22-year-old mistress, Marie-Therese Walter. Picasso was 55 at the time.

I've been fascinated by the painting since the Las Vegas casino mogul and art collector Steve Wynn stuck his elbow through the lower right corner back in 2006, thus squelching a deal he'd made to sell the painting to hedge-fund gazillionaire Steven Cohen for $139 million. Wynn paid $90,000 to fix the tear, then reportedly sold it to Cohen a second time, in 2013, but now for $155 million.

When a friend of mine saw an early version of the cover with the painting, she remarked, "You do know, I'm sure, that Picasso painted an erect, uh, how shall I put this, uh, an erect, uh, *member* as part of Marie-Therese's face?"

"Of course," I quickly replied. "Everyone knows that."

I had no idea. I consulted Wikipedia first thing, and sure enough, there in the second paragraph no less, how Picasso had "painted an erect penis, presumably symbolizing his own," in the face of his model. This prompted one art critic to suggest that, given the fact that the appendage in the painting is anything but erect, and given Picasso's age at the time, and that of his mistress, the title of the painting should perhaps have been "Wishful Thinking."

Of course, now when I see the painting, I don't see anything else.

No doubt Picasso's studio was a mess….

October 1, 2015

Dale Bridges

Dale is a fiction writer, essayist, and freelance journalist living in Austin, Texas. His writing has been featured in more than thirty publications including *The Rumpus*, *The Masters Review*, and *Barrelhouse Magazine*. He has won awards from the Society of Professional Journalists for his feature writing, narrative nonfiction, and cultural criticism, and his essays and short stories have appeared in a number of anthologies. His debut short story collection, *Justice, Inc.*, was released in 2014.

Read an excerpt from *Justice, Inc.* at <u>wewantedtobewriters.com/arcology</u>, or check out Dale's website, <u>dalebridges.org.</u>

About a year ago I started working at a used bookstore, which is a bit like an alcoholic getting a job at a winery. Temptation is everywhere.

Imagine the size apartment a writer/bookseller can afford, and then cut those dimensions in half. That's where I live with my wife and our psychotic cat, The Tempest. We have three bookshelves that are crammed to bursting, but that doesn't stop me from creating tome towers in every room, disjointed, Jenga-like constructions that appear stable but crash to the floor if you look at them funny.

We don't have a bed, per se, but there's a mattress on the floor in the bedroom and an ever-changing tome tower on my side that The Tempest pushes onto my head whenever the little serial killer gets bored. The stack contains new books I'm enjoying for the first time and old favorites that I re-read pathologically.

Amy Falls Down is the latest novel by the incomparable **Jincy Willett**. I feel like a Bible salesman when I talk about Willett. So few people have heard the Good News, and I desperately want to convert them. *Amy Falls Down* is a dark, sharp-witted satire of the publishing industry. Willett skewers everyone from online trolls to radio commentators to elderly Norman Mailer-wannabes. I love this book.

If I manage to convert someone to Willettism, I then move on to Richtianity. *Twin Study* is **Stacey Richter**'s second short story collection, and it is a flawless combination of postmodern satire, pop magical realism, and good ol' fashion storytelling. No other fiction writer makes me shoot vodka out of my nose like Richter.

I've been reading a lot of short story collections lately. I know they're passé, but there's no better place to find exciting new voices. **Okla Elliott**'s *From the Crooked Timber* is one of those wonderful small-press books that make you ache with anticipation for what's to come next from the author. These are gritty stories filled with physical and psychological trauma, but there are small rays of sunlight if you look hard enough.

There are no such sunny moments so far in **Jim Thompson**'s *Savage Night*, however. I'm only about fifty pages into the novel, but from past experiences with Thompson I'm not going to hold my breath. Thompson was written off as just another pulp fiction writer during his lifetime, but he's become something of a cult figure since his death. I wouldn't want to live in a Thompson universe every day, but it's a damn entertaining place to visit.

Posted June 20, 2014

David Corbett

David Corbett is the author of five novels: *The Devil's Redhead*, *Done for a Dime*, *Blood of Paradise*, *Do They Know I'm Running?*, and the just-released *The Mercy of the Night*. His short fiction and poetry have appeared in numerous magazines and anthologies, with pieces twice selected for *Best American Mystery Stories*, and his non-fiction has appeared in the *New York Times*, *San Francisco Chronicle*, *Narrative*, *Zyzzyva*, *MovieMaker*, *The Writer*, *Writer's Digest*, and numerous other venues. He has taught through the UCLA Extension's Writers' Program, Book Passage, LitReactor, 826 Valencia, The Grotto in San Francisco, Delve Writers, and at numerous writing conferences across the US, and in January 2013 Penguin published his textbook on the craft of characterization, *The Art of Character*.

Find out more on David's website at davidcorbett.com, or read an excerpt from his latest at wewantedtobewriters.com/arcology.

Austin Wright, *Tony and Susan* — The most gripping, unusual, elegantly written fiction I've read in some time. (Sadly the author, a former lit professor at the University of Cincinnati, died before the recent re-issue of this previously overlooked novel could gain for him and the work the audience and respect it deserves.) Though "postmodern mysteries" too often trend toward the over-precious and self-absorbed, this one delivers in a very fundamental, even insidious way. Ex-husband Edward, after twenty years of separation, sends remarried ex-wife his manuscript about a man whose wife and daughter are abducted, raped, and murdered along an empty stretch of Pennsylvania freeway. The book-within-a-book is riveting, but it's Susan's response to what she didn't know about Edward, and thus herself, that lifts an otherwise excellent read to the level of the unforgettable.

Dennis Lehane, *World Gone By* — Although this book is the third in a trilogy, I read it first, and now intend to go back and read the others. Lehane referred to this effort as "The Gangster in Autumn," and that's apt, for it plays in a minor key, elegantly so. I was prepared to enjoy the story but not be quite so blown away. A few sections are so expertly crafted I went back and re-read them before going on. No one with his roots as firmly planted in realism as Lehane writes as imaginatively, with the seemingly fantastic conveyed so gracefully, so credibly, that you can't help but tell Mr. Disbelief to take the night off. Lehane's confidence as a storyteller has never felt more assured, and the scenes between father and son convey an emotional impact so heartbreaking that it lifts this novel high above its would-be counterparts in crime fiction.

Lady Augusta Gregory, with an introduction by William Butler Yeats, *Gods and Fighting Men* — Blame *Game of Thrones* for this selection and the next. I downloaded this book off the Internet and have been having a grand old time just paging through it slowly. The stories, which range from the account of how the Tuatha de Danaan came to inhabit Ireland to the classic tales of Finn McCumhal and the Fianna, are rowdy, blustering, bawdy, mysterious, tragic accounts of how the old magic served and betrayed the fabled folk who once inhabited the Emerald Isle. Utterly addictive.

Royal Case Nemiah, *Selections from Ancient Greek Historians in English* — I've had this book since I picked up a used copy for fifty cents at Long's Bookstore, where I worked while attending Ohio State, but I only started reading Herodotus recently, at the suggestion of Stuart Archer Cohen, a writer friend whose most recent novel, *This is How It Really Sounds*, is also on this list (see below). Again, blame *Game of Thrones* for getting me into offbeat history, and if "The Mythical Causes for the Wars Between Greece and Persia" doesn't apply, nothing does. "And thus commenced, according to their authors, the series of outrages," i.e., the abductions of Io and Europé and

Medea and Helen. "Now, as for the carrying off of women, it is the deed, they say, of a rogue; but to make a stir about such as are carried off, argues a man a fool."

Jill Leovy, *Ghettoside*: *A True Story of Murder in America* — A gripping, maddening, heartbreaking look at the two worlds of justice—black and white—in present-day Los Angeles. The author, a reporter for the *Los Angeles Times*, argued to her editors that every murder in the City of Angels should be noted in its flagship paper. This launched her on a journey of discovery into the largely forgotten and routinely unsolved killings of young black men in South Central. If not for the dogged, heroic efforts of one man, a (white, Republican) detective named John Skaggs, those murders would slip beneath the surface forever—especially the murder of Bryant Tennelle, whose death forms the centerpiece of this sad, brave book.

Janine Wedel, *Unaccountable: How Elite Power Brokers Corrupt Our Finances, Freedom, and Security* — A bit of a slog, and there are times the outrage doesn't quite feel commensurate with the alleged crimes, but gradually I've come to realize that's the point. The complete transformation of power in the US into a system of elite insiders beyond the reach of voter accountability has been such a sly, seemingly reasonable shift that no one seems to have noticed. It makes the old cash-for-favors corruption look almost quaint, and its largely meritocratic veneer shields it from the condemnation it deserves. This book is too careful and meticulous to present a cry from the ramparts, and the interconnections of influence can often seem just like the old buddy system—what's the great sin? But as I've been reading it I've wondered why we haven't been more outraged by the conspicuous disappearance of decision-making beyond closed doors, or any responsibility for consequences.

Stuart Archer Cohen, *This Is How it Really Sounds* — The author is a friend, and this is the one book I've not yet actually read, but which is the next book of fiction I intend to get to. Stuart's always believed in breaking down walls, and he refuses to be tamed by reader expectations—and yet he's an utter gas to read. Here he follows the stories of three powerful men all named Peter Harrington—one an extreme sports hero, another an aging rock star, another a pirate financier. Each has severe regrets, each finds his life in miserable disorder, each seeks that ever-elusive reason for being. I can't wait.

Posted May 1, 2015

Lucille Lang Day

Lucille Lang Day is the author of a memoir, *Married at Fourteen: A True Story*, which received a 2013 PEN Oakland Josephine Miles Literary Award and was a finalist for the 2013 Northern California Book Award in Creative Nonfiction. She has also published a children's book and eight poetry collections and chapbooks, including *The Curvature of Blue*, *The Book of Answers*, and *Infinities*. Her short stories, poems, and essays have appeared in more than 100 literary magazines, such as *The Cincinnati Review*, *The Hudson Review*, *The Paterson Literary Review*, and *The Threepenny Review*. The founder and director of a small press, Scarlet Tanager Books, she also served for many years as the director of the Hall of Health, an interactive museum in Berkeley.

Find out more on her website, lucillelangday.com, or Twitter, twitter.com/LucilleLDay.

The books by my bed are always a mix of ones I've recently read and have yet to put away, ones I'm currently reading, ones I want to read, and ones I've already read but want to take another look at. Here's what's in the pile today:

Patricia Damery and **Naomi Ruth Lowinsky**, editors, *Marked by Fire: Stories of the Jungian Way* — Damery is a novelist, Lowinsky a poet. Both are Jungian analysts. Lowinsky's first two poetry collections, *Red Clay Is Talking* and *Crimes of the Dreamer*, were published by my press, Scarlet Tanager Books, and I have read all of her previous and subsequent books except *Marked by Fire*, a collection of personal essays in which thirteen Jungian analysts describe the life-transforming experiences that led them to the Jungian path. So far, I have read only the first essay, Patricia Damery's "The Soul is a Riddlemaker: Three Lessons." In this story, Damery analyzes a mysterious dream in which she must find a manitou, which appears in the dream as a large black bird but also turns out to be, Damery learns in her waking life, a spirit or force that permeates the natural world in some Native American religions. This is a tale of dipping into the source of one's spirituality and creativity, and one does not need to be a Jungian either to appreciate it or to learn from it. I certainly will read the rest of the book.

Daniel J. Langton, *Personal Effects: New and Selected Poems* — Langton, who teaches English and creative writing at San Francisco State University, was encouraged by William Carlos Williams, but his poetry is more reminiscent of Robert Frost's. *Personal Effects*, his seventh poetry collection, contains many sonnets and other poems written in form, but Langton makes these forms his own. He has invented a subtle sonnet rhyme scheme (ABCD/ABCD/EFG/EFG) that he uses to great effect. The insights of these sonnets range from the political ("There is a tax on flowers where I live") to the philosophical ("Life teaches, art reminds") to the startlingly wise ("we know who's dying, not who's being born"). All of the poems, whether free verse or formal, display a narrative sense that is often conspicuously absent in contemporary poetry and introduce us to characters—some real, others fictional—we come to care about. The poems are accessible, and I believe they will prove engaging to people who don't usually read poetry as well as to those who do.

Susan Gubernat, *Arroyo Literary Review*, Spring 2014 issue — *Arroyo* is an annual literary journal published by California State University East Bay. It is edited by graduate students working under the direction of Gubernat, faculty member and poet. Christopher Morgan edited the 2014 issue. Because I serve on *Arroyo*'s advisory board, I am always eager to read it in order to confirm that this is indeed a journal in which I want my name to continue to appear. It has never disappointed. The many excellent poems and stories in the 2014 issue include Alan Feldman's "What the Pig Meant," a poignant poem about memory loss, and Dallas Woodburn's "Goosepimples," a short story that upends the politically correct victimization narrative by showing us a young girl who tries to seduce her soccer coach.

Stephen D. Gutierrez, *The Mexican Man in His Backyard: Stories & Essays* — I first read this book in manuscript form and wrote a blurb for it: "Illuminating the beauty and confusion of Mexican American life in Los Angeles and Fresno from the 1960s to the present, the stories and essays in *The Mexican Man in His Backyard* are simultaneously personal and universal. Stephen Gutierrez captures a particular culture in particular places and times, but he also probes many themes—such as aging, death, parenthood, coming of age, and workplace politics—that are relevant to everyone. The characters are memorable and the stories linger, causing tears or laughter long after the book is closed, the last word read." In this collection, the distinction between "story" and "essay" is blurred. Some of the pieces were originally published as personal essays, others as short stories. I find myself going back to them and asking myself, *What is a story? What is an essay? What is fiction? What is nonfiction? Why does it matter?*

Michael Stocker, *Hear Where We Are: Sound, Ecology, and Sense of Place* — This book was a gift from a friend who heard the author speaking on the radio. She thought it would interest me (and she was right) because I have studied biology and worked as a science writer and science educator. This book inverts the familiar premise that sound is something that conveys information and affects the listener. Yes, it does these things, but there is another way of thinking about sound, and the inversion results in a focus on sound as something that humans and other hearing animals use to establish relationships with their surroundings. It also reveals sound as an important aspect of place, just like visual imagery. I learned all of this just by reading the back cover. Now I want to know the details of how it works, so I look forward to the book.

Alicia Suskin Ostriker, *The Old Woman, the Tulip, and the Dog* — I just started reading this new poetry collection by Ostriker, whose work I have been following for about forty years. The many subjects she has eloquently addressed in previous books include childbirth and motherhood, aging, the nature of love, and the search for God. The poems in the new collection, which appear simple but are exquisitely crafted, feature three characters (you guessed it: the old woman, the tulip, and the dog) who reflect on everything from the nature of a blessing to the sight of deer on a hillside to the experience of drinking to promises to oneself, just for starters. I expect these characters to take up many significant questions of the sort Ostriker has always grappled with. Giving the dog the last word, the poems are wise, witty, and philosophical. They are also so much fun to read that I will sign off now so that I can get back to this book.

Posted July 11, 2014

Polly Dugan

Polly Dugan is the award-winning author of *So Much a Part of You*, which writer Alan Heathcock said "announces the arrival of a potent and fresh new voice" in fiction. Her second book, *The Sweetheart Deal*, was published in 2015 by Little Brown & Company. A former employee of Powell's Books, she is an alumna of the Tin House Writer's Workshop and a reader at *Tin House* magazine. Her short fiction has been featured as a *Narrative Story of the Week* and awarded an Honorable Mention in *Glimmer Train*'s Short Story Award for New Writers contest. She lives in Portland, Oregon.

Find out more at Polly's website, pollydugan.com.

The next best thing to binge-reading authors I love—Paul Auster, James Herriot, John Irving, Stephen King, Carolyn Keene, and Nancy Drew—is reading a succession of great books by different authors. It's not an easy or likely thing to accomplish, luck-wise. I'm sure I'm not the only reader to have been deeply affected by a book, to absorb the characters and their plights and carry them around with me, only to have the next book I start pale by comparison for simply suffering the bad timing of being the book with the tough act to follow.

So I felt extremely lucky this summer, around the time my book was published, to discover not one or two, but four books that delivered story and language and reader investment in such a way that I couldn't help but picture all four of them together raising the bar high as a team, creating a very daunting height indeed. Of the four, two of the books were new to the world, and the other two were simply new to me.

The first was *The Land of Steady Habits* by **Ted Thompson**. As a college student, I was an avid fan (and binge-reader) of **John Cheever**—that red mass market, *The Stories of John Cheever* was so easy to take with me *everywhere*—and Thompson's book reminded me so much of the complicated, conflicted, privileged, and tragically comic characters who populate Cheever's stories. It's thoroughly brilliant. I sent a note to Ted after I'd finished reading it, telling him that, as a reader, I wanted to immediately go back and read it again, and as a writer, it was a book I wish I'd written myself.

The next two books I picked up were *Mary and O'Neil* by **Justin Cronin** and *The Blessings* by **Elise Juska**. Though they were published over a decade apart, both books had been floating around in my periphery, popping up in my Friday *New York Times Book Updates* email or another outlet, and so I'd listed them on my to-read post-its. And then in June two reviews very generously made some comparisons between *The Blessings* and my linked story collection, *So Much a Part of You.* For years I'd had my eye on Cronin's book because of the acclaim it received, including being a Hemingway Foundation/PEN Award recipient, and after having written a book in the same form—Cronin's is billed as "a novel in stories"—I love to see how other writers work within that structure. And, the form is one of my personal favorites. I consumed Juska's and Cronin's books in the most perfect way: reading until your eyelids surrender and you simply cannot read another word, and so you fall asleep with the book open, right there to pick up when you awaken the next morning.

Both Juska and Cronin channel the deep spectrum of human emotions in such a way that it seemed I *knew* the people in these novels, and that I had *felt* their experiences. My experience was a thoroughly visceral one; while reading both books, I didn't so much weep as sob. One afternoon I read Cronin's book right up until the very minute I had to leave the house to pick up my kids from school. I did the best I could to clean up after my tears, lest another parent misinterpret and assume I'd just come from receiving bad news. I took Juska's book with me to one of my son's fall baseball games. I kept opening and closing the book, allowing myself time to collect myself and appreciate my immersion in it, prompting my husband to ask if I was okay. Both books contain an abundance of the beauties and struggles of life, the ways the human spirit prevails over the unavoidable losses we endure, the challenges and gifts of family.

Both Juska and Cronin (and Ted Thompson too) have mastered writing diverse points of view. They are equally sure-handed and authentic across genders, ages, and stages of life and circumstance. If you read any portion of either of their books without knowing who wrote it, guessing whether the author was female or male would be a gamble.

And finally, both Juska's and Cronin's books resonated with me because from the first pages I recognized their characters: *These are my people*. Both books are based in or connected to Philadelphia and the northeast, where I hail from, and the Irish Catholic Blessing family is like so many I knew as a child, teenager, and young adult. There was a comforting sense of "going home" reading these books because the writing in both captured distinct regional details. There's a beautiful line in Juska's book about how a character's accent reveals they are from the area. It's subtle and small and if you're not familiar or haven't experienced the same thing—as I have—you might miss it.

After three books, I thought my lucky streak had run out. But then I read *This Is Where I Leave You* by **Jonathan Tropper**. Just in the way Juska, Cronin, and Thompson peel back the lives of WASPS and Irish Catholics, Tropper drops you in the room—in some cases in the chair—with a grieving Jewish family sitting shiva and makes you privy to all their quirks and flaws and histories. In many ways Tropper's voice reminded me of **Jami Attenberg**'s in *The Middlesteins* or **Steve Almond**'s in *Which Brings Me to You* (which he co-wrote with **Julianna Baggott**). All three writers rely on humor—really laugh out loud stuff—to diffuse the tragedy/loss/heartbreak their characters are battling. There's nothing irreverent or dismissive about successfully pulling off tragicomedy; it's an advanced maneuver. Throughout *This Is Where I Leave You* I was consistently moved, amused, and impressed. All the good page-turning stuff is there—infidelity, sex, marriage, parenting, siblings politics, gifted young men who seem invincible but in fact aren't.

When I finished my winning reading streak and thought about it, I realized what all these books share—perhaps the singular reason I loved them all—is that they're stories about families, told with naked candor, empathy, compassion, and without apology. But ultimately the pathos is balanced with redemption and resilience. That's the stuff for me, there's nothing better.

Posted January 9, 2014

Grant Faulkner

Grant Faulkner is Executive Director of National Novel Writing Month and the co-founder of 100 Word Story. His stories and essays have appeared in *The New York Times*, *Poets & Writers*, *Writer's Digest*, *The Southwest Review*, *PANK*, *Gargoyle*, *eclectica*, and *Puerto del Sol*, among dozens of other journals. His collection of one hundred 100-word stories, *Fissures,* was released in 2015.

Find out more about Grant and his work on his website, grantfaulkner.com. Read an excerpt from *Fissures* at wewantedtobewriters.com/arcology.

The interesting thing about my reading life is how messy and sprawling it's gotten. When I was younger, I seemed to read with greater focus, reading only two or three books at a time, and reading them much more quickly than I do now.

I don't think "messy" and "sprawling" have to carry negative connotations, though. The sprawl is good because I'm curious, so my reading is wide-ranging and somewhat unbridled. Perhaps more importantly, I'm increasingly moody, so I need to have a variety of books in motion to match the finicky needs of my odd and unpredictable states.

As a result, I have several stacks of books, all contending to be read, like children asking for a parent's attention. These are the books that have made it out of the confines of a small bookshelf I purchased solely to prioritize the books to be read next on my list. I wonder if there will someday be a structure for yet another tier of books classified as "to be read after the 'to be read' books are read."

Some of the books in my pile will be read and read again. Some paged through and dismissed. Some will never be read, or I'll reach out for them just as I die, and say, "But…"

Books that accompany me to the front porch on moody Saturday mornings:

I like to drift on Saturday mornings. That first hour of the day is somewhat sacred because I know it will soon be eclipsed by life concerns, whether it's a child's soccer game or even the business of writing. I want my thoughts to traipse gently, and without any determined direction, like the fog that I'll sometimes find on one of the perfect mornings when I stow myself away on the bench on the front porch.

So I read things that inspire drifting. I've been reading **Frank O'Hara**'s *Lunch Poems*—both because it's the 50th anniversary of the book and because I like the curious meandering of O'Hara's mind as he walks about town noticing things. I've spent many a lunch in my lifetime trying to reclaim the poetry of my mind on a dreary day of work.

John Berryman's *Dream Songs* also often accompanies me. I'd initially planned to read one dream song a day this year (there are 385), but my peripatetic reading style took over, so it might be more of a two-year project.

And then I'll often wisp through *A Lover's Discourse* by **Roland Barthes**, picking up an idea or a phrase to riff on in my journal. Barthes is perfect to drop in and out of. I'm almost always reading something by Barthes.

The books in my satchel:

These are the books of the day, the books that accompany me on commuter trains and trips.

I decided that re-reading is as important as reading books for the first time (and perhaps more important), so I'm now re-reading *Tender is the Night*, my favorite book by **Fitzgerald**. I haven't read it in 25 years or so, and since it's a novel partly about the passing of youth, I thought it would be interesting to inhabit Dick Diver's demise now that I'm an older man.

I recently got the fortuitous chance to spend an evening with **Peter Coyote**, a remarkable man of much wisdom and many experiences. I'm reading his memoir, *The Rainman's Third Cure*, which explores his life and his mentors. We can never have enough mentors, and it's an interesting exercise to identify and reflect on my own mentors.

And then I try to keep one book on writing going at all times, so I've been re-reading **Lewis Hyde**'s *The Gift: Creativity and the Artist in the Modern World*. It's a comforting book for a writer like me, who doesn't expect to make any money from writing, but approaches it with almost religious purpose.

The books that go on for years:

I love books about alcoholic writers. If I were abandoned on a deserted island and had to choose a short list of books, they'd all be by and about that wonderful pantheon of gloriously reckless and doomed alcoholic scribes. Someday I'd like to teach a course on novels written by alcoholics.

I just finished *Cheever: A Life*, **Blake Bailey**'s amazing biography of John Cheever. I'm now reading Cheever's letters, the collection of all of his short stories, and I plan to read his journals, of course.

I've heard it said that writers nurture their anguish, burnishing it daily with their words. That anguish can be such a strange friend or enemy, an endlessly interesting spiritual center. Cheever held such anguish, a secret that guided and crippled him. Yet perhaps it also made life a much more interesting affair.

Books that taunt me:

If I ever read **Hermann Broch**'s *The Sleepwalkers*, I should treat myself to a trip to Paris. Or perhaps I should treat myself to a trip to Paris just to read it. It's been staring at me for years.

It seems unlikely that I'll read **David Foster Wallace**'s *Infinite Jest*. I'd like to take a poll of the number of people who own *Infinite Jest* and have read it. I think the percentage would be low.

I wonder how I can die without reading **Proust**. That defines the injustice of life, that I might die without reading Proust. But there he is, waiting, whispering that there will never be a perfect time to read him, so I should read him now.

The books that are next:

After *Tender Is the Night*, **James Salter**'s *Light Years* awaits re-reading. I've heard **Virginia Woolf**'s *The Waves* described as a prose poem, and I'm very interested in thinking of the novel as a prose poem because that seems to be the way I'm most inclined to write.

On that note, I can't wait to read **Peter Matthiesen**'s *Far Tortuga*, a story pieced together in fragments. And then there's **Jenny Offill**'s *Dept. of Speculation*, written in a similar manner. Since I write flash fiction, and am increasingly drawn to an aesthetic of brevity, I plan to write a novel that is essentially a collection of little shards pieced together.

Posted May 8, 2015

Wendy Fox

Wendy J. Fox's debut *The Seven Stages of Anger and Other Stories* won the Press 53 award for short fiction, and her stories have appeared or are forthcoming in *Washington Square*, *The Pinch*, *ZYZZYVA*, *The Tusculum Review*, *The Puritan*, and many other literary journals. Her novel, *Deals*, is forthcoming from Underground Voices in 2016. She lives in Denver.

You can find out more about Wendy on her website, wendyjfox.com and Twitter, twitter.com/WendyJeanFox. Read an excerpt from her short story collection at wewantedtobewriters.com/arcology.

I'm a bad bedtime reader—I get started and then wake up later with the light still on and my glasses mashed against my face, the book open to the same page, now dented and drooled on. Still, I like the bedtime stack because it's the last thing I see before sleep and the first thing I see when waking up. If I am going to really read it, the book needs to migrate out to daylight. Here are the ones that have recently made it:

Midge Raymond, *Forgetting English* — This was a re-read. *Forgetting English* came out from Press 53 in 2011, and just after it hit, a friend (the poet and essayist Janée J. Baugher) scanned one of the stories and emailed it to me with a note that implored me to read the rest. I took her advice, and recently, when I was working through some new stories of my own, I revisited this collection. Raymond's writing is so clean, and I admire how she weaves elements of corporate life into elements of the natural world. In particular, "The Ecstatic Cry"—the story my friend first scanned—is a standout; I mean, how do you set something in Antarctica and have it ring true? Raymond handles the setting and the characters so deftly, you feel like you too could learn to love the cold.

Polly Buckingham, *The Florida Review* — This fiction chapbook is 60-ish pages from *The Florida Review.* What I admire about Buckingham's prose is the extreme attention to detail, and that the detail is always doing (at least) double duty. Here's one of my favorite passages because so much happens and we learn so much in the space of a few sentences:

> When he'd first visited his parents after her death, his father had given him a box full of his old tools. There were well cared for antiques, their wood handles worn from use, and they worked with greater precision than most pricey new tools. He'd wept in his father's workshop, the most orderly room he'd ever known, surrounded by the sweet smell of sawdust, the metal table with forty tiny labeled drawers, and the old wooden paper cutter Charlie had loved as a child. His father held up gracefully against his tears. He put another log in the woodstove, handed Charlie a cup of black coffee, and they sat in silence listening to the crackling of the fire.

Maybe it's not fair to make these four sentences speak for the whole work—which is why it is worth reading the rest of it.

Gregory Spatz, *Inukshuk* — I didn't read this when it first came out in 2012, but I read it on a long plane ride after I saw in the news that one of the ships from a mid-1800s expedition in the Northwest Passage had been discovered by the Canadian government. The *HMS Terror* and the *HMS Erebus*, caught in the arctic ice along with the men who sailed them, are the backdrop for the novel. I loved this book because Spatz is able to ground a desperate, terrifying journey with contemporary characters, and it successfully balances a very fine line between commercial and literary fiction. Since finishing it, I keep waiting to hear news of someone selling the screenplay. The images from the discovered shipwreck are haunting, but Spatz's novel is just as visual, paired with spot-on dialogue and a family with just the right amount of mess.

John Keeble, *The Shadows of Owls* — I've hardly cracked this book, but so far it reads like vintage Keeble—I feel like his characters are always set at the scalding point, in the sense of how the word is used in cooking: that controlled space just before a boil. In the opening, we meet Kate, and I suspect she may keep me up all night.

Posted January 30, 2015

Clifford Garstang

Clifford Garstang is the editor of *Everywhere Stories: Short Fiction from a Small Planet*, a new anthology from Press 53. He won the 2013 Library of Virginia Literary Award for Fiction for his novel in stories *What the Zhang Boys Know* (2012). He is also the author of a story collection, *In an Uncharted Country* (2009), and the editor of *Prime Number Magazine*. After receiving a BA in Philosophy from Northwestern University, Garstang served as a Peace Corps volunteer in Korea. He earned an MA in English and a JD, both from Indiana University, and practiced international law in Singapore, Chicago, and Los Angeles with one of the world's largest law firms. Subsequently, he earned a Master of Public Administration from Harvard University's Kennedy School of Government and worked as a legal reform consultant in Almaty, Kazakhstan. From 1996 to 2001, he was Senior Counsel for East Asia at the World Bank in Washington, D.C. He holds an MFA from Queens University of Charlotte and currently lives in the Shenandoah Valley of Virginia.

Check out Clifford's website at cliffordgarstang.com. Find out more about *Everywhere Stories* on Facebook at facebook.com/everywherestories. You can read an excerpt at wewantedtobewriters.com/arcology.

At any one time, I have a lot of books going and many more waiting in the wings. So what's on that list right now?

I'm currently reading *The Sixth Extinction*, by **Elizabeth Kolbert**. This is a frightening presentation of the disastrous effects humans have had on the planet. By now we all know about the asteroid that crashed into the earth and caused the mass extinction of the dinosaurs and many other species. Basically, humans are having the same kind of impact as that asteroid. That's not a cheery thought, but it's a fascinating book.

I'm also reading *The Great Glass Sea* by **Josh Weil**. I've known Josh for a while, and we did a joint reading several years ago when our first books came out. This book is terrific—set in a near-future Russia, about two brothers and the consequences of orbiting mirrors that bring constant sunlight to a vast greenhouse. The language is pure poetry, and so far at least the story is extremely engaging.

While I'm on the subject of fiction, I'm also in the middle of an audio version of *The Man with the Golden Arm* by **Nelson Algren**, which won the National Book Award in 1950. It's a gritty drug-scene story set in post-war Chicago. It's great for the dialogue alone.

I often have one book of poetry going, also, and that right now is *Memory Chose a Woman's Body* by **Angela M. Carter**. Angela is in a writers' group that I facilitate and her poetry is confessional, unflinching, and usually a bit dark. She says that poetry saved her life, and you really get that feeling from reading the poems.

I also usually have a book of philosophy or spirituality going as well, and now I'm reading **A. J. Ayer**'s *The Problem of Knowledge*. I read some of this in college, too, and it's every bit as dense as I remember it being, but I'm a big fan of logic and understanding the difference between facts and beliefs, so this is right up my alley. Plus—although it sounds a little odd—it's research for a novel I'm working on.

Let me also mention a few good books I've recently finished that haven't yet found their way to a spot on the bookshelves (assuming I can find some room):

Dust to Dust by **Benjamin Busch** is a memoir that spans his childhood (Busch is the son of beloved novelist and short story writer Frederick Busch) and his military service in Iraq. I enjoyed the book for its candor and its structure, which is built around basic elements—water, metal, soil, bone, and so on.

Another recent non-fiction read that I admired was *Whistling Vivaldi* by **Claude M. Steele**. Steele is a social psychologist who has long studied the way in which "stereotype threat" (basically the fear of confirming negatives about one's group, especially gender and racial stereotypes) creates a performance gap that can be mitigated with appropriate cues and a supportive environment. Apparently, it's that easy.

I also recently finished a historical novel by **Maud Casey**, *The Man Who Walked Away*, set in the early days of European psychoanalysis and dealing with the peculiar relationship between a doctor and his patient, a man who frequently wakes up to discover that he's wound up in some unfamiliar city.

And the last poetry book I read was *Until You Make the Shore* by **Cameron Conaway**, which I picked up and had signed by the author at the AWP Conference earlier this year. The collection stands out because it is in the voices of four young women in a juvenile correctional facility where Conaway once taught. It should be performed as theater (as I've told the author).

Which leaves the books I'm looking forward to next:

I just got a copy of a collection of stories by **Elizabeth Kadetsky** (mysteriously identified only as "Kadetsky" on the cover) called *The Poison that Purifies You* that looks really intriguing. With many of the stories being set abroad, it's just the kind of thing I enjoy.

I've been meaning also to read *The Orphan Master's Son* by **Adam Johnson**, which won the Pulitzer Prize. It's set in North Korea and because I lived in South Korea for two years as a Peace Corps volunteer in the '70s, I'm sure to find this one really interesting. (And, I have a novel set partly in Korea that my agent is trying to sell.) So that's the next novel I'll tackle.

My book club is reading **Dr. Carl Hart**'s *High Price*, which is a neuroscientist's book about drug addiction—from someone who has been there, apparently. I'm looking forward to that one.

Posted October 24, 2014

Kathie Giorgio

Kathie Giorgio's fourth book, a novel called *Rise From The River*, was released in early 2015 and debuted at Carroll University, where she was visiting author. The book has been chosen for the Top Five Must-Reads of Spring by Boswell Books and was included in the Top 100 Must-Reads of Summer by the *Milwaukee Journal Sentinel*. Her third book, the novel *Learning To Tell (A Life)Time* (2013), debuted at the Southeast Wisconsin Festival of Books to a standing room only crowd. Her first novel, *The Home For Wayward Clocks* (2011), received the Outstanding Achievement award from the Wisconsin Library Association and was nominated for the Paterson Fiction Award. Her short story collection, *Enlarged Hearts* (2012) was selected by the *Milwaukee Journal Sentinel* as one of the 99 Must Reads of that summer. She is the founder/director of AllWriters' Workplace & Workshop.

Find out more about Kathie on her website, kathiegiorgio.org, and on Facebook at facebook.com/kathie.giorgio. Read an excerpt from her latest at wewantedtobewriters.com/arcology.

A while back, I thought to organize my home and office by making a special place for those books that piled up by my bed…by my couch…on my kitchen island…in the bathroom. I have shelves in my office, just behind my desk. One afternoon, I cleared one out and then put my waiting books there. Success! I had room for four vertical piles of books!

Well, until that filled up. Last week, I took the books that were stacking up precariously on my desk and put them in what I thought was an artful sculpture by my window. I've seen home decorating articles and HGTV shows with books incorporated into room design. In my office, though, it just blocked the sun. But it's worth it. Books are life.

Here's a sample of what's in my window stack and how

they came to be there.

Anne Tyler, *A Spool of Blue Thread* — Years ago, when I was still writing fantasy, I was introduced to the art of literary fiction through Anne Tyler. The first book I read of hers was *The Clock Winder*. I find it to be kismet that my first published novel was called *The Home For Wayward Clocks*. Tyler grabbed me by the wrist and firmly tugged me onto the path of realistic stories with a lovely twist—quirky characters that are oh-so-human. In all of Tyler's books, she toes a careful tightrope. Her characters are real, but different, unusual, but believable, not so out there as to be impossible. They're people we'd like to meet on the street, but maybe not have in our homes indefinitely. This year, I was delighted when she released a new novel, *A Spool of Blue Thread*. Because Tyler is who Tyler is in my life, I didn't even read the synopsis before I bought it. As soon as it was announced, it was pre-ordered, and now it rests in my window pile.

Paul Torday, *Salmon Fishing in the Yemen* — Tyler came to me through my mother's recommendation. But the next book, *Salmon Fishing in the Yemen*, came to me through a movie trailer. I don't even remember what movie I was there to see, but the trailer came on and the title alone was enough to get me. Who would go fishing for salmon in the Yemen? Just as a title will get to me, so will lines of dialogue. During the movie, the following conversation takes place:

> *Sheikh Muhammed: You're not a religious man?*
> *Dr. Alfred Jones: No. No, I'm not.*
> *Sheikh Muhammed: But you're a fisherman, Dr. Jones.*
> *Dr. Alfred Jones: I'm sorry, I don't follow.*
> *Sheikh Muhammed: How many hours do you fish before you catch something? Dozens?*
> *Dr. Alfred Jones: Gosh, hundreds sometimes.*
> *Sheikh Muhammed: Is that a good use of your time for a facts-and-figures man? But you persist in the wind and the rain and the cold with such poor odds of success. Why?*

Because you're a man of faith, Dr. Alfred.

And I sat forward. I thought, how many hours do writers write before they see any breath of success? And I thought, writers, *all* writers, religious or not, have to be the most faith-filled people I know. I went home and ordered *Salmon Fishing in the Yemen*. It's in my stack. I will read it until I see what Torday actually said in the book. I can't wait.

Ron McLarty, *The Memory of Running* — Right at the moment, in this window stack, there are two books by Ron McLarty, and there is another one, *Art In America*, on my kitchen island, as I'm currently reading it. McLarty came to me through a used bookstore. I was browsing through the clearance books and came across his *The Memory of Running*, and its stunning cover. What attracted me was not "running" in the title, but a bicycle in the cover art. I needed to know how that connected, and so the book came home with me.

The Memory of Running is one of those rare books that you carry with you everywhere so that you can read it with every spare second you have. I read it while I waited to pick up my daughter from school. I read it at stop signs. I read it as I climbed up and downstairs in my home, when I went into the bathroom, when I had two minutes between clients. Like Tyler, McLarty is a master of the quirky, but real character. The cameo appearance in this book by an artist drawing in chalk on a sidewalk in a big park in New York City is nothing short of amazing. The artist only appears on a few pages. But when she leaves, we know her entire life.

This caused me to go out and buy everything McLarty has written. As I said, I'm currently reading *Art in America*. In my window pile, I have *Traveler* and *The Dropper*. I may hold on to *Traveler* until I travel by train to Portland, Oregon this summer (44 hours on a train!). It seems fitting.

Leslie M. Rupracht, *Splintered Memories* — And sometimes, voices bring me to books. The last time I wrote about my *Books By the Bed*, I was traveling to North and South

Carolina. In North Carolina, I was the featured reader for Main Street Rag Publishing Company's Final Friday reading series. After I did my part, I sat, drank wine, and took in the words of other writers, all poets. One of those poets was Leslie M. Rupracht. At the mic, Leslie flexed her lyrical muscle and raised her voice. Her work was strong and soft, at once simple and complex. The hallmark of a poet. I was entranced.

So when her poetry collection, *Splintered Memories*, came out, I believe I was first in line to buy it. That voice, strong, soft, complex, simple is here on every page. An example from her poem, "Lingering":

> The palm of my hand
> A memory rests briefly
> Takes flight to the past

See what I mean? A moment of simplicity—a single memory rising up—leads to the complex—a trip to the past. Just lovely. Leslie's book rests on my window stack now, but will soon move to my bedside table, so I can read some of her poetry every night before I go to bed. That voice will lull me to sleep, but lead me to dreams. Simple to complex.

It's so hard to say what draws someone to a book. Covers, movies, voices, history. All I know is I keep getting drawn. My shelf behind my desk isn't going to suffice. The window stack will grow larger. If I hope to have any sun at all, I'd better build a wall.

Posted June 12, 2015

Kathy Girsch

Kathy Girsch lives in Oregon with her husband Bill and Murphy, their yellow Lab. A nature lover, creative cook, avid traveler, and international film enthusiast, she counts reading as her number-one passion. She has been a nonstop reader all her life, and she was fortunate to have teachers who encouraged her to expand her horizons by reading eclectically. Ultimately her love of reading led her to pursue an MA in Spanish Literature, an undertaking which broadened her world view and diversified the contents of her bookshelves.

My books by the bed are on side tables all over my house: by my bed, by the sofa where I sometimes fall asleep at night, and next to the leather chair in the den. I'm a fanatic reader who falls in love with authors, places, and, above all, characters. While I'm in a relationship with one or more of these lovers, I am obsessed. I plow through my bookshelves researching everything related to the above-mentioned people and places, and then I dream about them; I re-read paragraphs until they're memorialized in my heart. Here are some books that are close to the top of the stack right now.

Anthony Doerr, *All the Light We Cannot See* — I'm almost halfway through this surprise 2014 bestseller, which takes place during WWII in France and Germany. The short chapters carry the reader backward and forward in time with rapid shifts between characters and countries. I've fallen in love with Marie-Laure, the blind protagonist and even more so with her father, who cares for her so tenderly, so pragmatically. I love reading about how Werner, a German orphan, uses his innate genius for radios, math, and science to open his world. A lot of the action takes place in Saint-Malo, a French city I'd not heard of before starting this book, so I've spent plenty of time reading about it and its role in WWII. I'm looking forward to filling several more evenings with these characters as they make their way through the horrors of the war.

Sharon Salzberg, *Loving-Kindness: The Revolutionary Art of Happiness* — It's a book on Buddhist thought and practice that I read last summer, and I keep going back to it. In a simple, absolutely refreshing way this compassionate author offers just the right message to a recovering Catholic who's always seeking redemption and reconciliation.

Harold Bloom, *Shakespeare: The Invention of the Human* — This book, which re-examines each of Shakespeare's plays through the lens of a true Shakespeare lover, has had a place by my bed for more than 10 years; I haven't finished it and don't expect to do so, but I have read and reread sections of it with a vengeance. The author's passionate interpretation of the plays and their characters never fails to fascinate me. Lately, it's Hamlet who has caught my attention, and Bloom's ability to reveal Hamlet's "infinite variety" and his inexplicable charisma simply rocks.

James Carroll, *Jerusalem, Jerusalem* — I fell in love with this author as I was attempting to read *Constantine's Sword* (never finished it but I do expect to some day). In *Jerusalem*, Carroll goes back to prehistoric times as he relates the history of monotheism. He explores the actual and metaphorical history of Jerusalem; follows the intertwined threads of Judaism, Islam, and Christianity; and carries us right up to the present-day problems in the Middle East. As always, Carroll matches his scholarship with emotional engagement, and that's what I love about his writing.

Rosa Montero, *Pasiones* — This is another book I keep around to reread whenever I feel like it. The author deftly examines the intense passions of 18 famous couples from Antony and Cleopatra, through the Duke and Duchess of Windsor, on to John and Yoko, and it's impossible not to become a third party in their relationships. I'd love to share it with more friends, but it's not available in English.

Hilary Mantel, *Wolf Hall* — Last but not least. From August until October this novel about Thomas Cromwell filled my days and my nights. I cherished it so much that I couldn't read it quickly. I wasn't familiar with Cromwell when I started the book, but this intelligent, energetic, coldly practical—yet warmly loving—character captured me in the first few pages and wouldn't let me go. A complaint of some readers was that the use of a third person limited narrator instead of the expected—and easier to follow—first person narrator was needlessly confusing (who is "he" anyway?). This device took some getting used to, but I came to see the wisdom of using third person to tell the story; it allowed the author to praise Cromwell without having the character seem self-aggrandizing. My husband thought I might go into withdrawal upon finishing the book, but as long as it's available for me to reread from time to time, I'll be fine.

Posted January 23, 2015

Kate Gray

A rower for years, Kate Gray coached crew and taught in an East Coast boarding school at the start of her teaching career. Now after more than twenty years teaching at a community college in Oregon, Kate tends her students' stories. Her first full-length book of poems, *Another Sunset We Survive* (2007) was a finalist for the Oregon Book Award and followed chapbooks, *Bone-Knowing* (2006), winner of the Gertrude Press Poetry Prize and *Where She Goes* (2000), winner of the Blue Light Chapbook Prize. Her debut novel, *Carry the Sky*, was released by Forest Avenue Press in 2014. Over the years she's been awarded residencies at Hedgebrook, Norcroft, and Soapstone, and a fellowship from the Oregon Literary Arts. Her poetry and essays have been nominated for Pushcart prizes. She and her partner live in a purple house in Portland, Oregon, with their sidekicks, Rafi and Wasco, two very patient dogs.

Check out Kate's website, kategraywrites.com, for more about her and her books. Read an excerpt from her latest at wewantedtobewriters.com/arcology.

The books by my bed break my heart with their rich descriptions of the places they explore. Living in the Pacific Northwest, I recognize our setting as our most pervasive form of spirituality, and our writing tends to pay homage. What I often find in the books that strike me the most is a place described with such presence it walks within the characters. An essay that helps writers recognize the importance of place is Dorothy Allison's "Place" written for the Tin House Summer Writer's Workshop this July 2014. In it she defines place as… "not just what your feet are crossing to get to somewhere. Place is feeling, and feeling is something a character expresses. More, it is something the writer puts on the page—articulates with deliberate purpose." She tells us with the examples she uses that place breaks the reader's heart. She instructs: break your reader with details.

Carter Sickels, *The Evening Hour* — In his award-winning novel, Sickels does just that. He tells his story through the eyes of a young man who is trapped by poverty and his loyalty to his grandmother and the land they live on. The story reveals the rape of West Virginia by coal companies. The description of the setting caught me by the throat. In the novel a coal company levels mountain ranges, poisons land and water, and swindles communities. On one level the action of the novel revolves around a massive landslide due to the effects of clear-cutting, gutting the mountain by dynamite, and building flimsy dams that are overrun with toxic runoff. While the narrator is deeply flawed, it is his decency and generosity toward the most isolated and destitute in his community that redeem him. The writing captures the complexity of characters and economics, the choices made and the ones imposed.

> Ten days later he drove his mother and grandmother to Rockcamp to see what was left. On the way, they passed by yards where sofas and mattresses and toys and knick-knacks were laid out, drying in the sun. As they got farther away from Stillwell they saw heaps of trees, the remains of houses. Blackened craters were cut out of the land, like burnings. Nothing looked like it could be saved.

From this book I learned more about the ways that people get stuck, stuck where they live, stuck in cycles that seem from the outside breakable, but aren't.

Nancy Slavin, *Moorings* — In this novel, the place is as present as the characters:

> Many of the small Alaskan fishing towns along the Inside Passage have looked just as water-stained and run down as this, . . . with only a few people milling along docks and waving their way past piles of snowdrifts. The snow, she notices, is old, end-of-the-season snow, the kind that

exhaust fumes from car engines have spotted black, mixed in with months' worth of gravel and dirt and soot. But the town looks to be what she'd expected, weathered and full of stories.

The story about discovering the complex nature of family secrets is intricate. The writing is layered with detailed descriptions that bring to life not only the ways that families reveal and heal, but also the way that landscapes can be devastated and renewed.

Both of these books will transport you out of your house and into a landscape you may have never known before. The writers will break your heart in a good way, by helping you understand deeply the importance of lightening our impact on the land and deepening our impact on each other.

Posted September 12, 2014

Stefanie Paige Gunning

Stefanie Paige Gunning is a Creative Director at MRY in New York City. She blogs at Working Without a Net (check it out at workingwithoutanet.wordpress.com) and is currently at work on an essay collection about marriage and parenting.

I do not remember learning to read. It has always seemed like a biological process, involuntary and essential. Consuming a story, absorbing a character—here was wisdom and pleasure, grief and sustenance, delivered a word at a time.

I learned how to be a person from books. They taught me about love, and heartbreak, what it is to be destroyed and redeemed. Books are how I found family, understanding, and friends. They were my way forward in the world. And they are the way I mark time, the events of my life inextricably tied to what I was reading at any given moment, my own history unfolding alongside the teetering stack of books by my bed.

The books I remember most from childhood are the ones I sneaked off my mother's bookshelf and read clandestinely when I ought to have been asleep. I tore through **Judith Rossner**'s *Looking For Mr. Goodbar*, *Attachments*, and *Emmeline* in a hot rush when I was 11, and swooned willingly into a dark, delicious underworld of fatal one-night stands, graphic sexual liaisons with co-joined twins, and incest. I hated being a child, the helplessness of it, and the dependency. And here was adulthood, laid out in all its glittering darkness.

As a teenager, the stack by my bed was a lavender-scented shrine to angst and longing, terror and drama. **Sylvia Plath**'s *The Bell Jar* atop **F. Scott Fitzgerald**'s *The Great Gatsby* atop **J.D. Salinger**'s *The Catcher in the Rye* atop **ee cummings**' *Selected Poems 1923-1958* atop **W.H. Auden**'s *Collected Poems* atop **Pablo Neruda**'s *Twenty Love Poems* atop **Walt Whitman**'s *Leaves of Grass*. **Stephen King**'s *The Shining*, *The Stand*, and *The Dead Zone*. **Ray Bradbury**'s *Fahrenheit 451*,

The Martian Chronicles, *Something Wicked This Way Comes*, and *The Illustrated Man*. **Roald Dahl**'s *Kiss Kiss*.

In college, my interests turned to the theatre, to the Transcendentalists, to mythology and world religions. My mattress was on the floor then, in an actual writer's garret I rented in an old Victorian house. I filled that room with paper and ink, bourbon and books and cigarette smoke. I read into the small hours of the morning, tucked under a thick down comforter my mother sent when she realized I was deadly serious about living in a drafty room in upstate New York in the middle of winter. My bed was ringed by tomes on Christianity, Judaism, Buddhism, Hinduism, Islam, and Taoism. There were at least three versions of the Bible. **Joseph Campbell**'s *The Power of Myth*. **Homer's** *The Odyssey* and *The Iliad*. The collected works of **Ralph Waldo Emerson**, **Henry David Thoreau**, **Nathaniel Hawthorne**, **Walt Whitman**, and **Henry Wadsworth Longfellow**. **Shakespeare**. **Aeschylus**, **Sophocles**, **Euripides**, **Aristophanes**, and **Aristotle**. Hundreds of slim plays from Dramatists Play Service. I directed **Lee Blessing**'s *Eleemosynary* my junior year, and I still have the production book I made.

My 20s were a lost decade, a watercolor wash of depression, debilitating anxiety, a misguided marriage to my college boyfriend, and our brutal divorce. I stuffed myself with books during those years, desperately trying to feel something, anything. Of the hundreds of books I read, a few stand out vividly. I read and re-read **Kurt Vonnegut**'s *Slaughterhouse-Five*, adopting the tragic comfort of "so it goes" as a mantra. I found **Wally Lamb** in those years, and took solace in the self-engineered redemption of Delores Price in *She's Come Undone*. **Jeanette Winterson**'s *The Passion* held out a gossamer hope that there might still be a passionate love waiting for me, somehow. **Ursula Hegi**'s *Stones From the River* gave me courage. **Donna Tartt**'s *The Secret History* felt like a long-lost friend, one who spoke my language of wasted youth.

I started my 30s single for the first time in my adult life, living alone in a quirky Brooklyn brownstone apartment, fragile from the emotional slaughter of dismantling the life I shared with my now ex-husband. I was made of glass, all eyes. I went to therapy. I went to the gym. I slept with a lot of men, some of them kind, others not so much. And I read. Wally Lamb again, at first, losing myself in the raw emotion and reassuring bulk of *I Know This Much Is True*. And then women authors, for the first time really, a rich diet of female voices that nourished me like bone broth. **Anne Lamott**'s *Traveling Mercies* showed me there was a writer inside me. **Jennifer Weiner**'s *Good in Bed* made me laugh out loud with tears streaming down my face, for here was a chubby Jewish girl with boy troubles and Daddy issues, and my God, how I could relate. I gathered women writers to me, filled my house with them—**Ann Patchett**'s *Bel Canto* and her best friend **Lucy Grealy**'s *Autobiography of a Face*, and then Ann's story of their friendship and Lucy's death, *Truth & Beauty*. **Margaret Atwood**'s *The Handmaid's Tale*, *Cat's Eye*, *The Robber Bride*, *Alias Grace*, and *The Blind Assassin*. **Toni Morrison**'s *Beloved* and *Jazz*. **Alice Walker**'s *The Color Purple*, *The Temple of My Familiar*, and *Possessing the Secret of Joy*. Poet **Wislawa Szymborska**'s *People on a Bridge* and *View With a Grain of Sand*. **Anna Quindlen**'s *One True Thing* and *Black and Blue*. **Diane Ackerman**'s *A Natural History of Love*, **Jane Smiley**'s *A Thousand Acres*, **Anita Diamant**'s *The Red Tent*. **Helen Fielding**'s *Bridget Jones's Diary* did what I believed to be the impossible—it let in a little light. It made me feel better.

I am in my mid-40s now, married to a man whose goodness takes my breath away, the mother of a daughter who is the purest joy I have ever known. The stack of books by the side of my bed has been replaced by a Kindle, a device I find wondrous for the way it inexhaustibly feeds my voracious hunger for reading. But there are still books in my house, to serve as talismans. I have five copies of **J.D. Salinger**'s *The Catcher in the Rye* with the red cover, a small collection, but one that gives me deep pleasure. I am still touched by Holden Caulfield, his vulnerability and sadness. I keep **Harper Lee**'s *To Kill A Mockingbird* nearby, Atticus Finch standing in for the father I longed for as a child. A copy of **E. Annie Proulx**'s *The Shipping News*, inscribed by the man who gave it to me, the first man I loved after my divorce, whom I still think of with such affection. I have Auden's poetry on my shelf, and cummings', and Neruda's, and Whitman's—the same copies that sat on my bedside table in high school. **Dorothy Parker**'s *Complete Poems* and *Complete Stories*. My old college copy of Joseph Campbell. I run my hands over them sometimes, and think of how we've traveled, how far we've come.

Right now I am reading **Anne Lamott**'s *Small Victories*, a meditation on forgiveness and renewal, transformation and love. I read late into the night still, my Kindle light aglow, my husband asleep beside me, my daughter tucked into bed down the hall. I read, and I am full.

Posted December 5, 2014

Therése Halscheid

Frozen Latitudes, Therése Halscheid's fifth poetry collection, has been awarded The Eric Hoffer Book Award, Honorable Mention for Poetry. Her other collections are *Uncommon Geography*, *Without Home*, and *Powertalk*. She received a Greatest Hits chapbook award by Pudding House Publications. Her poetry and essays have appeared in such magazines as *The Gettysburg Review*, *Tampa Review*, *Sou'wester*, and *Natural Bridge*. Since 1993, she has been an itinerant writer by way of house-sitting. Simplicity has connected her to the natural world and has been the focus of many poems. Her photography has appeared in juried shows and chronicles her nomadic lifestyle. She teaches for Atlantic Cape Community College in New Jersey, visits schools, and has taught in unusual locales such as an Eskimo village in northern Alaska, and the Ural Mountains of Russia.

Find out more about Therése and her poetry on her website, ThereseHalscheid.com, or on Facebook at facebook.com/therese.halscheid. Read an excerpt from *Frozen Latitudes* at wewantedtobewriters.com/arcology.

Recalling **Ernest Hemingway**'s *A Moveable Feast*, I'd like to at least borrow from his title and talk about "A Moveable Bedside." And that's not because I have so many, many, many lovers that I can't decide where to rest my tired head. It's because, well, I'm just a house-sitter. That's how I've been writing for several years. Traveling light is one sure way to keep the book stacks in check.

Usually when I journey, I consider location and what types of books I must have with me, to either coincide with my adventure or for pleasure reading, or to assist what I am working on. There are a few that fall into my traveling book bag, no matter what. One is **Lao Tzu**'s *Tao Te Ching*. This book—which gets placed on every night table—includes 81 timeless poems that teach me how to live. What is amazing about this 2,500 year-old text is how each poem's message continually evolves. I mostly use the book as a divination tool, by opening at random and focusing on the poem that is revealed. Then apply that wisdom to daily events. If I happen upon the same poem, the wisdom shifts although, of course, the words never do. I recommend this book because it will resonate with you, according to your own understanding. There is an interesting story about how the *Tao* was written. Lao Tzu was an old philosopher who kept observing the Chinese Provinces vying for supremacy, and he was growing tired of the rivalry amongst leaders of his time (sound familiar?). And so he decided to leave the city and live his life in the mountains. But it so happened the gatekeeper had received an oracle that suggested something important was coming his way, and that he should not let it pass. Along comes Lao Tzu on his oxcart and the gatekeeper, remembering the oracle, told Lao Tzu he was not allowed to leave until he shared all that he knew. It is said he parked in the grasses and there wrote his 81 poems, then handed them to the gatekeeper, rode off and was never seen again.

Another book-by-the-bed that has been a constant since its release is *Wild Iris* by **Louise Gluck**. The poetry astounds me on many levels, and I am not yet tired of learning from the collection. Gluck's poems are written in the language of flowers and yet there is hardly anything flowery about them. It is an ethereal collection, where flowers voice their observations of the human's world, or a flower offers something about itself, its purpose, or how it perceives the poet as gardener. These personae poems combine with others that are in the poet's voice, and all combine to address the poet's existence, her failing marriage. An interesting backstory of the writer's process comes from an interview I read where Gluck actually created this collection in one summer—over a brief period of six or seven weeks, I believe. The poems flooded out of her and she gave in to a rather overwhelming need to write daily.

An important essay collection that has been tagging along, to land upon these various bedside tables is *The Next American Essay*, an anthology edited by **John D'Agata**. The collection embraces essays that take creative risks: lyrical essays and stylistic hybrids in which form is just as exciting as content. The lyric essay is a form I am experimenting with, and I so enjoy being fueled by accomplished writers whose works are acknowledged. Essays in this collection are as varied as their authors and include Annie Dillard, Joan Didion, David Shields, Susan Griffin, John McPhee, Barry Lopez, among others.

Am I allowed to include my relatively new iPad, and my recent inclination to download books? The Pad most definitely shows up beside my bed(s), and even finds its way onto the pillow(s). Its pink rubbery case flips back to expose a luminous text. Because this is a new way to read, I have but a few titles to share. One is **Annie Dillard**'s *Pilgrim at Tinker Creek* and **Joan Didion**'s *The Year of Magical Thinking*. And—though I'm not sure why—I suddenly wanted **Dostoevsky**'s *Notes from the Underground* one night. These are books I can read without lamplight, or tiny contraptions that work as flashlights that clip to a bedrail and bend any way you want.

That's all? you might ask. Not really. This is what I currently have on my person. What of other books? Well, luckily I can resort to bookshelves in the attic that was once my childhood bedroom. There is a family residence that I visit, and frequently pluck something off the old shelf. I've also been invited to read books in the homes I care for. This has exposed me to art books and literature that I would not have selected on my own. And magazines—it's always good to drop the latest issue of *The Writers Chronicle* or *Poets & Writers* or *The New Yorker* into the traveling book bag, and plop them atop the bedside heap—or a contributor's copy of journals in which my work has appeared. These magazines are as exciting as works by a single author. They broaden my world. I learn of others whose works I might not have known in any other way.

There are books that remind me of my life on the road.

They are visitors of a place. Recent visitors include: *Truth & Beauty* by **Ann Patchett**, *Autobiography of a Face* by **Lucy Grealy**, *From Our House* by **Lee Martin**, and *Townie* by **Andre Dubus III**. Seems I have been reading memoirs of late, because I am currently focused on nonfiction.

"If you are lucky enough to have lived in Paris as a young man, then wherever you go for the rest of your life, it stays with you, for Paris is a moveable feast." This Hemingway quote inspired the title for his posthumous memoir. I feel the same about books—wherever you go, no matter what the bed or bedside—a good book remains inside you!

Posted November 7, 2014

Tara Ison

Tara Ison's memoir, *Reeling Through Life: How I Learned to Live, Love, and Die at the Movies*, was released in early 2015 by Soft Skull Press to glowing reviews. Tara is also the author of the novels *The List*; *A Child Out of Alcatraz*, a finalist for The Los Angeles Times Book Prize; and *Rockaway*, selected as a 2013 Best Books of Summer by *O Magazine*. Her short fiction and essays have appeared in *Tin House*, *The Kenyon Review*, *Nerve.com*, *Publishers Weekly*, and numerous anthologies. She is co-author of the cult film *Don't Tell Mom the Babysitter's Dead*.

Learn more about Tara on her website, taraison.com, Facebook, facebook.com/taraisonwriter, and Twitter, twitter.com/taraisonwriter.

Right now, the books by my bed are:

Peter Turchi, *A Muse and a Maze: Writing as Puzzle, Mystery, and Magic* — Full disclosure: Pete Turchi is a former colleague and dear friend of mine, but no one writes as beautifully, joyfully, and cleverly about the process of writing as he does. I'll quote: "Turchi draws out the similarities between writing and puzzle making, reading and puzzle solving. He distinguishes puzzles (which can be solved) from mysteries (which can't) and teases out how a combination of the two can lead to something like magic—the creation of credible illusion." And the book itself is gorgeous, full of illustrations and maps and diagrams—you know how some books just *feel* rich? I can't wait.

Hilary Mantel, *Bring Up The Bodies* — Last time I wrote one of these guest posts, I was struggling to get through *Wolf Hall*—as I said, I'm a Tudor porn junkie, and I should have loved this psychologically insightful, exquisitely written, historically accurate drama… yet I found it a slog. For some reason, I now feel obligated to work my way through this sequel. (I suspect it might simply be because I'm excited about the forthcoming mini-series…sigh…)

Helen Humphreys, *Coventry* and *The Lost Garden* — She's a Canadian novelist and poet I think doesn't get enough attention. I adored two other novels of hers: *Wild Dogs* and *Afterimage*. She writes slim, poetic novels that take your breath away. Once I was at a restaurant with one of her books for company and I stumbled onto a sentence that made me gasp with pleasure — I called the waitress over to read it to her, because I had to share it. I don't even know what these two are about, and I don't care. Read her.

And I also need to catch up with books by some of my Counterpoint/Soft Skull Press siblings: *Gangsterland*, by **Tod Goldberg**, *Refund*, by **Karen Bender**, and *The Object Parade*, by **Dinah Lenney**. Wonderful writers, all of them!

Posted January 16, 2015

Pam Jenoff

Pam Jenoff is the internationally bestselling author of *The Kommandant's Girl* and several other novels. Her latest novel, *The Last Summer at Chelsea Beach*, was released in mid-2015. Her short story "Strand of Pearls" was in the anthology *Grand Central: Original Postwar Stories of Love and Reunion*. Pam was a former diplomat with the State Department, political appointee at the Pentagon, and attorney. She lives outside Philadelphia with her husband and three children where, in addition to writing, she teaches law school.

For more about Pam, check out her website at pamjenoff.com.

True confession #1: I don't actually have books by my bed—or anything to put them on. We moved into our house three weeks before the twins were born. It's been four years since then and with three preschoolers we've yet to hang a picture or buy furniture. The bed is just mattress, box spring and frame, and there isn't enough light to read. So I'm just as liable to be found reading on the sofa or in the tub or in the big comfy chair by the bedroom window, if I can manage to clear all of the piled clothes from it.

True confession #2: I don't hang onto books. I get them from the library, or buy and read and pass them on. I just don't have the space. The house is overflowing with books that have pictures and rhyme. So I grab books anywhere I can, but I don't necessarily have them for long.

With the disclaimers done, the books in my metaphorical stack by the bed include:

Susan Elia MacNeal, *The Prime Minister's Secret Agent* — I've actually been reading all of the books in MacNeal's Maggie Hope series. This is the fourth and latest installment about a young American woman doing work for the British government during the Second World War. I tend to read books set in the same period in which I am writing to see how they capture the time and place and MacNeal just nails it.

Lisa Barr, *Fugitive Colors* — I met Lisa on tour for the Jewish Book Council last year and she is a remarkable woman so I had high expectations for her book—*Fugitive Colors* has far surpassed them. It is the story of artists in Paris and Berlin on the eve of the Second World War, and it is explosive and vivid.

Mary Kubica, *The Good Girl* — Mary is a debut author from my publisher, Mira, and her book has been getting such fabulous buzz as the next *Gone Girl*. I met her at Book Expo this year and she and **Heather Gudenkauf** were just terrific. (Heather is the author of *Little Mercies*, which is also fabulous; I'm only not including it here because I already finished it.)

Sarah McCoy, *The Baker's Daughter* — This book, which goes between World War II Germany and the present day, is next up on my list. Sarah and I were both authors in the anthology *Grand Central: Original Postwar Stories of Love and Reunion,* which came out in June and when we met at the launch in New York City, it was sisterhood at first sight with her and Jenna Blum and the others. I'm trying to work my way through books by the other nine *Grand Central* authors and I've heard great things about this one.

Blake Snyder, *Save the Cat!* — Okay, admittedly this is an outlier, but I do love books on writing craft. Snyder's work is aimed at screenwriters but his advice on plot is so strong that I've heard great things about it from many novelists.

And finally, there are a number of books not yet "by my bed" because I haven't been able to get my hands on them yet, but I'm quite excited to read *Lucky Us* by **Amy Bloom**, *Lisette's List* by **Susan Vreeland** and *Close Your Eyes, Hold Hands* by **Chris Bohjalian**.

Posted August 29, 2014

Nicole C. Kear

Nicole C. Kear is the author of the memoir *Now I See You*, chosen as a Must-Read by *People,* Amazon, *Martha Stewart Living*, *Parade, Redbook*, and *Marie Claire UK* among others. She is currently working on the first six books of an early reader series for children, *The Fix-It Friends*, to be published by Macmillan Kids' Imprint in 2017. Her essays appear in *The New York Times*, *Good Housekeeping*, *New York*, *Psychology Today*, *Parents*, as well as Salon, the Huffington Post, and xoJane, and she teaches writing at the NYU School of Professional Studies. A native of New York, she lives in Brooklyn with her husband, three children, and two aquatic frogs.

You can follow Nicole's continuing mis-adventures in motherhood on her blog, amomamok.blogspot.com, and learn more about her work on her website, nicolekear.com. Read an excerpt of *Now I See You* at wewantedtobewriters.com/arcology.

I read differently now that I've lost much of my vision. For starters, the printed page isn't much of a friend to me anymore; my cloudy, 40-years-ahead-of-schedule cataracts make the text blurry so deciphering the letters is always just beyond my grasp. E-books, however, are wonderfully accessible, since I can magnify the print until it's ridiculously big, which is usually when it's just right for me. And I've discovered audio books, too, which might just be the most momentous discovery of my lifetime, since they allow me to read while washing dishes and packing lunches.

It's not just going blind that's put a hitch in my literary giddy-up; having three young kids has changed things, too. A sizable chunk of my reading time now is devoted to reading to them at bedtime, and while there are definitely some low points (the phase when my son was obsessed with Backyardigans books was excruciating), there've been high points too, most of which involve me re-discovering, and sharing, the treasures of my childhood: *The Lion, The Witch and the Wardrobe; Little House on the Prairie; Beezus and Ramona*.

Because I have to steal time now to read, I'm far more discerning about what ends up on my figurative nightstand. Was a time I'd never abort mission halfway through a book, even when I was just trudging joylessly through; now, after a few chapters, if I'm not feeling it, I'll put it aside. Life's too short to read books you don't love. So all of these books currently in progress, are ones I genuinely love:

Madeleine L'Engle, *A Wrinkle in Time* — I've been waiting for years to read *A Wrinkle In Time* to my son; it was one of my all-time favorites when I was a kid. The experience of reading it again, twenty-seven years later has been really, really interesting. At first, I felt disappointed. It was slower, wordier, less engaging than I recalled. I was also terrifically impressed with 10-year-old me and with my son for grasping the huge, ponderous concepts broached, for braving the language—words like ineffable and ineluctable—and for having any idea at all what is going on in the story. Slowly, but surely, though, I fell in love with the book again, found myself right there with Meg every step of the way, rooting for her, daring to hope she'd emerge victorious. And at the book's end, I found myself sobbing, moved in such a profound way by the message of hope. When I was a child, the happy ending was a foregone conclusion, but as an adult, I felt so grateful for it, so overwhelmed by relief that things worked out OK in the end. I watched my son watch me cry—"Mom," he said, "You're nuts"—and I thought, "Just you wait."

Julia Fierro, *Cutting Teeth* — As mother to young children, I understand the potential of the playgroup to hold juicy intrigue. Send the playgroup on a weekend getaway to the beach and that intrigue will be unleashed in a hurricane of drama. I'm about halfway through and fully hooked; the book is just so honest about so much—about modern parenthood, about marriage, about friendship—and I am constantly arrested by how deeply moments resonant with me. It's the best kind of reading experience, one in which you want to squeal, "Oh my God, me too!!!" where the book feels like a great friend you just made. It's funny, too, and sexy as hell and I love that every chapter is told from a different character's perspective; it keeps things so dynamic and fun and makes it impossible to stop reading.

Karen Joy Fowler, *We Are All Completely Beside Ourselves* — I'm listening to this one as an audio book and it's seriously interfering with my productivity because I cannot will myself to hit the pause button. The book follows Rosemary Cook, who was raised with a chimp as a sister, as she tries to discover, and then understand, why her sister was taken from her when they were just five years old, and where she went. Except that a synopsis such as this doesn't really get to what the book is about. The book is about what it means to be part of a family, what it means to be human—and animal—what it means to love and to lose. There is so much I love about this book but what keeps me engrossed (I'm almost at the end now) is how much I adore the voice of the narrator. Rosemary Cook is so wicked smart, and truthful and just so damn funny; I want to have an old-school sleepover with her where we braid each other's hair and make friendship bracelets and stay up late telling secrets to each other. I want to have her zingy one-liners ("If stupidity were fuel, we'd never run out.") embroidered on throw pillows.

Rainbow Rowell, *Eleanor and Park* — I'm only a few chapters into this one but it's only because I've had criminally low amounts of leisure time of late. When all is said and done, there is no story I enjoy more than a love story, and of all the kinds of love stories, ones about young love are my favorite. My husband recommended this one to me, and I was sold as soon as I saw the cover. It's the kind of book you just fly through; you finish whole chapters without even noticing because it's such a joy to read and such an easy world to inhabit. But again, it's the characters that keep you rapt: the offbeat, wacky new-girl-in-school, Eleanor, whose family life is so screwed up it makes you wince, and the comic-book-loving music-junkie Park, who doesn't quite belong anywhere, either. It's funny, I half-thought that as I aged, I wouldn't enjoy reading about these super smart, effortlessly cool, and totally misunderstood teen characters, but it's just the opposite. As a parent, now, I love them all the more, and I feel really invested in what happens to them.

Italo Calvino, *Italian Folktales* — I bought this thick volume back when I was in college but it's just been taking up space on my shelf until it struck me as the perfect thing to read to my seven-year-old at bedtime. She has an abiding fascination for fairy tales—the more macabre, the better—and, as I suspected, these are exactly her cup of tea. I'm enjoying them too, finding them refreshingly absurd and shockingly dark. Our favorite story is a Cinderella narrative—except this abused, penurious sister falls into a hole in a garden where she meets a magical cat family that serve as her fairy godmother. When the vain, greedy, and all-around-abhorrent stepsisters fall into the same hole intentionally, they meet an entirely different fate, and while it may be a spoiler, I can't possibly resist telling you the cats force-feed them blood sausage until they die. It's not surprising that I relish a story like this but it is surprising that my daughter does. Surprising in the best possible way.

Posted August 15, 2014

Kim Korson

Kim Korson is a writer, originally from Montreal, Canada. Kim now lives in Southern Vermont with her husband and two kids, and says she doesn't get out much. Her memoir, *I Don't Have a Happy Place: Cheerful Stories of Despondency and Gloom*, was released in early 2015.

Read an excerpt of Kim's memoir at wewantedtobewriters.com/arcology. Her website is kimkorson.com. You can also follow her on Twitter at twitter.com/kimkorson.

I have a book buying problem. I don't want to say I'm a book hoarder, because most hoarders don't even use the things they pile on their dressers, beds, tables, and floors. Sometimes they buy items in duplicate, which I have only ever done with books *one* time, by accident. Sure, I purchase an overflow of books. But I read every single one. Eventually. They each earn a designated spot in my house. Books on writing get placed just outside my office on an old wooden shoe rack I scored from someone's trash in Brooklyn. Books that have been read get sent to the living room bookshelf. Research or titles similar to something I am currently writing go on my office coffee table. I always keep one in my purse and one in my car for when there are lines to wait in or kids to pick up at school. The rest lie in wait on my nightstand. Here's the current pile:

Celeste Ng, *Everything I Never Told You* — I am obsessed with debut novels, as well as all things 1970s-related, which is what first drew me to this title. Not to mention, the cover is terrific. This is a gorgeous novel, set in small town Ohio during the early '70s, about a Chinese American family dealing with the loss of one of their three children (the favorite daughter). Now, before you decide you can't read this because this subject matter is too upsetting, trust me when I tell you the tone of the piece is not overwrought or dripping with sap. This book is perfection. And it is a master class on point of view. I don't know how Ng slides from character to character so effortlessly—it's truly magic. If you haven't hoarded this one already, go get it and when you're done, pass it along to a friend immediately. I just did. I can't wait to get it back and read it again.

Barbara Trapido, *Brother of the More Famous Jack* — I haven't cracked this one yet but **Maria Semple** (*Where'd You Go, Bernadette* and other novels) adored it and that was all the recommendation I needed. Semple called it "breezy, raunchy and unsentimental." Turns out, it is also a debut novel. I don't even care what it's about; I love it already.

Alison Bechdel, *Fun Home* — I'm late to the party on this one but when I heard they were turning it into a musical, I knew I had to spend some time with it. This is a graphic memoir that explores Bechdel's complicated relationship with her father. It's dark and hilarious and depressing and gorgeous. We've all had moments when we look at our family and wonder how, and even if, we are related. I've never read a graphic memoir before but I know that what Bechdel has done here is profound and pioneering. I can't wait to finish and then go see the play.

Sharma Shields, *The Sasquatch Hunter's Almanac* — I confess I haven't opened this yet but the cover is divine. I bought this because it seemed bizarre, in the best way. It's the story of a nine-year-old boy who watches his unhappy mother walk into the woods with someone named Mr. Krantz, who may or may not be a sasquatch. Having been terrified and obsessed by Bigfoot as a child, I am eager to see how this is tackled.

Tom Perrotta, *Bad Haircut* — I read this book once a year. I don't remember where or when I bought it, but I cherish this copy and its contents. It's my first love of books. This is a collection of linked short stories, of a boy's adolescence during the 1970s. It's moving and funny and it's the very book that made me want to be a writer. I never lend out this copy so, if you haven't read it, I urge to go right now (right now) and buy it. You will not be disappointed.

Jonathan Tropper, *This is Where I Leave You* — A close second to Perotta is this book, with which I am also obsessed. When the family patriarch dies, the rest of the family is forced to sit shivah together in a house for seven days. This is the book I wish I'd written or could write.

And last but not least:

Ella Korson, *Don't Ask Me How it Happened* — Full disclosure, she is my ten-year-old daughter. She's still working on the draft so I can't divulge much but suffice it to say it was inspired by a hero to both of us—Judy Blume—and it is already chock full o' love and family and humor and heartache. Looks like my mothering work here is done!

Posted April 17, 2015

April Lindner

April Lindner is the author of three Young Adult novels: *Catherine,* a modernization of *Wuthering Heights; Jane*, an update of *Jane Eyre*; and *Love, Lucy,* a retelling of E. M. Forster's *A Room With a View*, all published by Poppy/Little, Brown Young Reader. She also has published two poetry collections, *Skin* and *This Bed Our Bodies Shaped.* With R.S. Gwynn, she co-edited the anthology *Contemporary American Poetry* for Longman's Penguin Pocket Academic series. A professor of English at Saint Joseph's University, she lives in Pennsylvania with her husband and sons.

Find out more about April on her blog at aprillindnerwrites.blogspot.com, and Facebook, facebook.com/AprilLindnerWrites.

My bedside bookpile is so huge that I've had to subdivide it. There's the books-I'm-actively-reading pile on my bedside table. There's the pile of the books I started actively reading but which got pre-empted for one reason or another; these are stowed under my bed. There's the books-I-hope-to-soon-be-reading pile, which sits downstairs, near the front door, so that I can pass it every day and feel a little bit guilty about the fact that I'm not reading fast enough. And then there's my Nook, which contains books from all three categories.

Books I'm actively reading:

David Levithan, *Every Day* — I just finished rereading this book for a class I'm teaching on Young Adult literature. I love the way this book marries the paranormal to contemporary realism—the ordinary high-stakes drama of teenage life. Our narrator—known only as A—is a genderless soul who wakes each morning in a different sixteen-year-old body. At the story's start, A falls in love with the girlfriend of a boy whose life A is inhabiting. The novel explores A's quest to be with that girl, despite difficulties that are at first merely logistical but then get ever more complicated and poignant.

Pablo Neruda, *Full Woman, Fleshly Apple, Hot Moon*, translated by Stephen Mitchell — I dip into these poems a few times a week, hoping I'll absorb some of Neruda's lush romanticism and exacting approach to the image. I've long admired Stephen Mitchell's translations which more often than most achieve true liftoff. Here's a delicious passage from "Ode to an Artichoke":

> *...scale by scale*
> *we undress*
> *its delight*
> *and we eat*
> *the peaceful flesh*
> *of its green heart.*

Books I was actively reading until I got distracted:

Mark Rotella, *Stolen Figs and Other Adventures in Calabria* — I like to torture myself by reading travel memoirs about Italy, a country I visit whenever I can and miss desperately the rest of the time. Rotella's vivid chronicles of his first visit to his ancestral homeplace in Calabria filled me with such intense wanderlust that I had to set the book aside, at least until the end of this last seemingly endless Pennsylvania winter.

Michael Wallner, *April in Paris* — I've actually got two copies of this book, one in English and one translated into Italian. For years now I've been trying to teach myself to read Italian by having both books open side by side and getting as far as I can in the Italian edition before cheating by glancing over at the original. (The farthest I've ever made it is a couple of sentences.) The story is fascinating. Roth, a young SS soldier/interpreter stationed in France changes into civilian clothes at night and slips out to mingle, incognito, among the Parisians. I've been tempted time and again to set down the Italian edition and just forge on ahead in English, to see how it all turns out. So far—even though the narrator has begun to fall for Chantal, a member of the Resistance—I've resisted temptation.

Books I soon hope to be reading:

Marlena De Blasi, *A Thousand Days in Tuscany* — More self-torture. Last summer I read *A Thousand Days in Venice*, in which De Blasi recounts how she fell in love with a Venetian stranger, married him, and moved to Venice. A few pages in, I fell in love too—with the author's quirky, poetic voice. I couldn't resist this sequel, in which De Blasi and her husband leave Venice to start a new life in Tuscany. I might have to pamper myself with limoncello and *spaghetti alle vongole* so I don't perish of jealousy.

Jon Skovron, *Man Made Boy* — This one looks like so much fun: a humorous retstaging of the Frankenstein story by one of my favorite Young Adult authors. Seventeen-year-old Boy, son of Frankenstein's monster and his bride, leaves the home of his overprotective parents for a road trip through the American heartland. I've been saving this one for summer.

Books on my Nook:

Donna Tartt, *The Goldfinch* — I've been submerged in the world of this book for about a month now. At 775 pages, it's my favorite kind of novel: thick, complex, wholly absorbing—the kind that makes the real world seem pale by contrast. Thirteen-year-old Theodore loses his beloved mother in a terrorist attack on the Metropolitan Museum of Art, and in a moment of blind panic escapes with a small Dutch masterwork in his backpack. The story follows Theodore through his troubled adulthood, deftly braiding its themes: love, loss, and the power of art. I'm about 120 pages from the end, and writing this makes me want to drop everything and read.

E.M. Forster, *A Passage to India* — This is the only one of Forster's novels that I haven't yet read, though I did see the

Merchant-Ivory film adaptation back when it first came out. I've been saving it, because I hate the thought of not having any of Forster's novels left to read for the first time. Many people believe it's his best, though it's hard to imagine anything surpassing *Howard's End*. I suppose the only thing worse than not having one last Forster book to look forward to is never getting around to reading that one last Forster book, so I plan to dig in soon.

Posted June 13, 2014

Jonnie Martin

Jonnie Martin is a native Texan, city-bred like the lead character in her literary western, *Wrangle* (nominated for the 2015 Will Rogers Medallion Award). Early in her career she was a journalist with a Texas newspaper before heading out to pursue a business career. Later she earned a BA in Literature/Creative Writing and an MFA in Fiction and returned to Texas, where she works as a novelist and a columnist for a newspaper, and blogs weekly on her website. In the long journey, she re-discovered her roots through her writing, drawn back to the land and the people who formed her.

Read her blog and her list of favorite westerns at jonniemartin.com. Follow her on Facebook at facebook.com/jonnie.martin.

Like every writer I have ever met, I began reading early and continue to devour books nonstop. I have always had a penchant for literary novels and in the past six years began to narrow my search to modern novels that have the markings of a classic. Three years ago, I narrowed my focus again, in both my reading and writing, toward literary westerns that might fit that description. That is a more difficult challenge.

Best of the Literary Westerns:

I keep a running list of my favorite literary westerns on my website and I find that these books mysteriously re-appear on my bedside table from time to time, requiring a new read. Here, I limit my notes to four books published after 1990—which unfortunately leaves out **Wallace Stegner**'s *Angle of Repose*, **Ivan Doig**'s *Dancing at the Rascal Fair*, and **Molly Gloss**' *The Jump-Off Creek*.

James Galvin, *The Meadow* — Galvin is primarily a poet, and writes a lyrical view of the 100-year history of a Colorado meadow at the base of the Neversummer Mountains. "The history of the meadow goes like this: No one owns it; no one ever will.... Only one of them succeeded in making a life here, for almost fifty years. He weathered." The book is a paean to the western way of life and as if it were not beautiful enough, he followed it with *Fencing the Sky*. Written with Galvin's usual poesy, *Fencing* is a dirge for the dying West.

Kent Haruf, *Plainsong* — When pregnant 17-year-old Victoria Roubideaux comes to live with two crusty old bachelors, Colorado ranchers Harold and Raymond McPheron, the men have no idea how to talk to her. They ask what she thinks of radio reports on market prices—commodities prices, that is—for cattle, soy beans, June wheat and pork bellies. Set in a fictional prairie town in Colorado, Haruf's ability to create laconic western characters on the page is remarkable. As the title *Plainsong* suggests, this book is a simple and beautiful song.

Cormac McCarthy, *Border Trilogy* — No one captures the brutality of the West like Cormac McCarthy, but this book is not gratuitous in its violence or oppressive in its mood—not nearly so dark as his Pulitzer-winning post-apocalyptic novel *The Road*. The book combines three of his prior novels that have linked stories of two teenage cowboys who search for the ranching lifestyle. The trilogy begins with the hopefulness of youth and ends with the stark reality of the dying West. McCarthy's direct style still conveys breathless moments of poignancy.

Denis Johnson, *Train Dreams* — A departure from Johnson's modern, edgy works, this novella follows a day laborer in the West in the early 1900s, a simple, uneducated man buffeted by loss and the violence around him. When he helps in the execution of a Chinese laborer caught stealing, he is horrified. Walking home in the falling dark, Grainier almost met the Chinaman everywhere. Chinaman in the road. Chinaman in the woods. Chinaman walking softly, dangling his hands on arms like ropes. I felt every blow to Grainier's safety and sanity.

Recently finished:

Brian Doyle, *Mink River* — Resplendent with Irish and Indian lore, the book is set in "A town not big not small. In the hills in Oregon on the coast. Bounded by four waters: one muscular river, two shy little creeks, one ocean." The people have similar, sad pasts; the Irish descendants still remember "The Hunger" that drove them to America; the Indian descendants still remember the lost lands of their ancestors, "The People." And while the histories live on in their minds and even in their language, this is not a bitter community, but a very human one.

Reading now:

I'm halfway through two books by first-time authors; both are memoirs; both have been noted by the *NY Times* and won awards; and both are stunningly excellent.

Domingo Martinez, *The Boy Kings of Texas* — A National Book Award finalist, this memoir vibrates with life and the stories of Martinez's will to escape his upbringing in a barrio in Brownsville, Texas, in "poverty so crushing that it leads to the death of his friends (*Texas Observer*)." Humor helps to alleviate the reality of this brutal existence.

Judy Blunt, *Breaking Clean* — Judy Blunt never set out to be a writer, but she is a natural, richly capturing the world of her homesteading family scratching to survive on the prairies of Eastern Montana. She grew up, married her cowboy, and did the unthinkable; breaking generations of family tradition, she took her children and left ranching life behind.

Waiting their turn:

William Faulkner, *Intruder in the Dust* — I came late to William Faulkner, a southern rather than western writer, but I live in Texas and we do have a drawl. I suspect Faulkner's *As I Lay Dying* will always be my favorite, but I reach back and read a different one of his novels from time to time, including this one of murder and racial divide in Mississippi.

Wendell Berry, *A Place on Earth* — Also a little off-course for me in my quest to find modern literary westerns, but I cannot resist the works of a poet and essayist like Berry, who captures in such rich details life in the forest and farmlands of Kentucky, and the stories of loss and redemption among simple folks of the land.

Posted July 4, 2014

Ilana Masad

Ilana Masad is an Israeli-American writer, reader, and editor living in NYC. She's been published in *The New Yorker*, *Printer's Row*, *McSweeney's*, Tin House's *Open Bar*, *Hypertext Magazine,* and more. She is also the founder of TheOtherStories.org, a podcast that features new, emerging, and struggling writers.

Find out more at ilanamasad.com and slightlyignorant.com, or on Twitter at @ilanaslightly.

Since acknowledging to myself fully that I am a writer, I've begun to read differently. If you're a writer too, you know how much hedging ("Well, I *want* to be a writer" and "I write, but I don't know if I'd call myself a *writer*, really" and "I mean, it doesn't really count, I just like writing") happens before you fully embrace that label. But once you do—or at least, once I did—I began to think of reading as an active participant in my writing, and this affected my reading habits.

In my teens, when I was still a starry-eyed actress-wannabe and math geek with a dying father, the books that were usually next to my pillow when I turned my light off at night were, in essence, storybooks. They were books that told good, developed, well-plotted, and well-written stories: **Tamora Pierce**'s *Song of the Lioness* quartet (and all her other books—I own them all and have read them many times); **Jacqueline Carey**'s *Kushiel's Dart* and its sequels (I read those too young and boy oh boy did they teach me a thing or two about sex); **Sarah Dessen**'s *This Lullaby* (and all her other books, which I still buy when they come out in paperback, because they provide a sense of simplicity in problem solving that I don't find in real life); **Jacqueline Wilson**'s *Girls Under Pressure*, which for some reason I read every time I was sick or had a migraine because there was something alluring about Ellie's bulimia (little did I know it would be even more of a solace to me later when I developed my own eating disorder). I'd endlessly reread my comfort books: **Gail Carson Levine**'s *Ella Enchanted*, *The Princess Diaries* by **Meg Cabot**, and, of course, the *Harry Potter* books, which were what got me started on this whole reading gig (it was pretty awesome to be 17 when the seventh book came out—I felt like I had literally grown up with Harry, aging along with him almost precisely).

Comfort books were and still are immensely important to me. One I bring with me wherever I move now is *Little Women* by **Louisa May Alcott**. I don't care if people say she hated writing it—I refuse to believe that. There is so much love, nostalgia, and wisdom in that book that it seems to travel through the years with me, like some fine wine that I get to drink over and over without destroying its aging process.

But now that I'm a writer, now that I admit I am one and consider myself one (though still with that sheepish artist shrug that conveys the "I know I'm never going to make any money" sentiment), I read for my writing as well as for the sheer joy of story.

Ulysses by **James Joyce**, a novel that terrified me for years and that I was basically conned into reading by a writing tutor at Oxford, was beside and in my bed for about four months. Reading it spawned my latest manuscript. **Virginia Woolf**'s *Mrs. Dalloway* has curled up with me on cold winter nights. But it's not only the dusty classics that have taught me how to write. I've had a steamy love affair with each of **Zadie Smith**'s books, from *White Teeth* to *On Beauty* to *Autograph Man* to *NW* (with some time along the way devoted to *Changing My Mind*, her book of essays) because of her gorgeous writing, her uncanny truth-telling, and her ability to create poignant, pathetic characters who are also unintentionally uproariously funny. I've cradled *The Amazing Adventures of Kavalier and Clay* and *Telegraph Avenue*, both by **Michael Chabon**, beside me and fallen asleep on them repeatedly, having read some of his sentences over and over, with my mouth hanging open, trying to figure out how he made them so crisp, clear and yet full of metaphor. I spent a solid year, two months, and one day with *Infinite Jest* by **David Foster Wallace** alternating spots between the kitchen table and my bed, adoring his run-on sentences, his ability to be funny and tragic and irreverent and soulful all at once.

Most recently, I've fallen in love with **Roxane Gay**'s *Bad Feminist*, and with **Taiye Selasi**'s *Ghana Must Go* and have embarked on *Land of Love and Drowning* by **Tiphanie Yanique**. Each of these women has a distinctive voice and point of view, and their writing sweeps me away, each very differently, and makes me want to write, write, write like the wind. I still do read for story (I've read all of Terry Pratchett, I love Neil Gaiman, and I recently swallowed whole **Paolo Bacigalupi**'s exhilarating and depressing *The Windup Girl*) and if I had my way, I'd spend most of my time doing nothing but reading. But I also want to keep learning how to write, which is a process that never ends, and so increasingly I challenge myself with writers who show me something new, who spin their yarns with a great deal of sentence-by-sentence thought, and who care about language for its own beautiful, dripping-off-the-tongue, clacking-in-the-teeth, echoing-in-the-mouth qualities.

Posted December 19, 2014

Felicia Mitchell

Felicia Mitchell grew up in South Carolina and North Carolina and then lived in Georgia and Texas before moving to rural southwestern Virginia in 1987 to teach at Emory & Henry College. She is a poet whose work has appeared in a variety of journals and two chapbooks. *Waltzing with Horses*, her first full-length collection of poetry, was published in 2014. In addition to publishing poetry and nonfiction, she has written articles for journals such as *College Composition and Communication*, *Mid-American Review*, and *Poets & Writers Magazine*. Edited projects include *Her Words: Diverse Voices in Contemporary Appalachian Women's Poetry*.

Find out more at Felicia's website, feliciamitchell.net, or on Facebook, facebook.com/ruthfeliciamitchell. Read an excerpt from *Waltzing with Horses* at wewantedtobewriters.com/arcology.

"By the bed" I will interpret loosely as I talk about books within the vicinity of my bed. Some books are *in* the bed, tucked inside an iPad, which I tuck into a pillow like a favorite doll before I fall asleep. My iPad has a dull gray, gull gray, cover, but inside are some colorful books. Right now, late in the evening, I am reading **Donna Tartt**'s *The Goldfinch*. I worry that this book will dematerialize before I finish it since I checked it out from the Washington County Public Library almost three weeks ago. Even if this book were made of paper, I would have to return it, though, and find a way to read on.

I like reading on a digital device. For me, it is as rewarding as reading a book with paper pages. Words take me into my imagination wherever I find them. I like being able to make the text larger, too, even with reading glasses making reading easier already. I like not knowing exactly what page I am on. What is not rewarding is the fact that when I am done, if I do buy the book, which I imagine that I will do with *The Goldfinch*,

I do not have a book to set aside in some stack in the house. There are stacks by the bed, stacks by the couch, stacks on the dining room table, stacks by the hearth but not too close to be a fire hazard. I cycle through these stacks, reading and sorting. I give away books all the time. I do not have an e-book buddy with whom to share e-books that I purchase (which is why I have started checking them out of the library now and then). Guilt—it is not difficult for me to feel guilty about something like having a book all to myself. I work around it.

There are other books on the iPad that I am reading now, after a fashion, since I rarely read one book at a time. This morning, I began the first chapter of my brother **C. Talmadge Mitchell**'s novel, *Dark Sings a Distant Herald: A Christmas Story on Holding Back the British Twilight*. Will this story come between *The Goldfinch* and me this evening? Even if it does not, I sense that I will not finish the Tartt novel in a few days. And there are more books in my bed. See below.

Then there are the books *beside* my bed. *The Essential Rumi* translated by **Coleman Barks** with **John Moyne** is always close at hand. Underneath that now is **Eckhart Tolle**'s *The Power of Now*, a book that I have been intending to read, now, any minute, since 1999. Perhaps I should sleep with it under my pillow and wake up enlightened. Or just open it every few years, which is my strategy, and continue on with my journey through it. Underneath that tome rests *Connected: What Remains As We All Change*, an anthology edited by **Heather Tosteson** and **Charles D. Brockett**, which includes my "Need Somebody to Love," an extended prose poem. I keep it near because this prose poem, just by being near, beneath the covers of that book, reminds me that sometimes I need to put the books down and go stand on the porch to watch the night sky.

Moving down the stack, I find *Central Appalachian Wildflowers* by **Barbara Medina** and **Victor Medina**; **Andrea Maloney Schar**'s *Your Mindful Compass: Breakthrough Strategies for Navigating Life/Work Relationships in Any Social Jungle*; and **Stanley L. Bentley**'s *Native Orchids of* *the Southern Appalachian Mountains. Your Mindful Compass* belongs to a friend who thinks it might help me become less reclusive. This book is in good company with *The Power of Now*. It reaches out to me: "Read me!" Sometimes I am just too busy living, or reading, to do that, although I have developed intimate relationships with a long list of other self-help books (another list waiting to be written down). Meanwhile, when I am not reading one book or ignoring another, or going on the porch to look at the night sky most nights, I am always learning something new about flowers (or birds). I am still trying to decide on an identification of a white orchid that I saw on the Appalachian Trail this past Monday. Great Plains Ladies' Tresses? Maybe so. The book will tell.

Other books residing inside the iPad and sleeping beside me most nights: **Lee Smith**, *Guests on Earth*; **Anuradha Roy**, *The Folded Earth*; **Matt Ridley**, *Genome: the Autobiography of a Species in 23 Chapters*; *Birds Illustrated by Color Photography 1897*; **Anne Tyler**, *The Beginner's Goodbye*; **Eben Alexander**, *Proof of Heaven: a Neurosurgeon's Journey into the Afterlife*; **Oliver Sacks**, *Hallucinations*; **Ann Patchett**, *State of Wonder*; **Barbara Kingsolver**, *Flight Behavior*; **Dan Silverman** and **Idelle Davidson**, *Your Brain After Chemo: a Practical Guide to Lifting the Fog and Getting Back Your Focus*; **Deborah Morris Coryell**, *Good Grief: Healing through the Shadow of Loss*.

I also have a hardback copy of *Flight Behavior*, which has managed to find its way to an actual bookshelf. Why two copies? I found myself at a conference wanting to finish this book, which I had left at home, and bought the e-book to read on my iPhone one evening when I was not out practicing being less reclusive.

Posted October 17, 2014

Mary Morris

Mary Morris is the author of fourteen books—six novels, three collections of short stories, and four travel memoirs, including *Nothing to Declare: Memoirs of a Woman Traveling Alone*. Recently her short stories have appeared in such places as *The Atlantic*, *Ploughshares*, and *Electric Literature*. The recipient of the Rome Prize in Literature, Mary teaches creative writing at Sarah Lawrence College. Her new novel, *The Jazz Palace*, set in Chicago during the Jazz Age, was released in 2015 from Nan A. Talese/Doubleday.

For more information visit her website at marymorris.net. Read an excerpt from *Jazz Palace* at wewantedtobewriters.com/arcology.

I have found a word in Japanese that perhaps most typifies my particular affliction when it comes to books. *Tsundoku*. It roughly translates to "someone who buys books and lets them pile up without reading them." I suffer somewhat from this trait. I buy books because I just must have them and then they sit around, sometimes for years, before I actually read them. The books at my bedside flow over to the dresser and then out into several piles stacked in the hall. There's a triage system going on here. The ones actually by my bedside are the ones I am probably actually reading at the time. The ones on the dresser are soon to be read or I've promised to read them. The ones in the hall have perhaps a sadder fate. It's a kind of literary limbo out there. I've already read them and they are waiting to be shelved (and may never be). Or they lingered so long by the bed that I felt guilty and moved them out of the way.

At my bedside at any given time there is always a pile of books. Or perhaps several. They fall roughly into three categories but they aren't organized in any particular way. There are the books I must read because I'm teaching them or as a favor to a friend, the books I'm reading because I'm doing research about something, and the books I want to read for pleasure (even as I ravage).

Right now beside my bed and beyond are *The Diaries of Christopher Columbus* (and they are fascinating), a book on the Spanish Holocaust, **Claudia Rankine**'s *Citizen*. I'm reading around in **Rick Moody**'s book of essays about music called *On Celestial Music*, and savoring **Maggie Nelson**'s exquisite *Bluets*. Also *Diaries of Exile* by **Yannis Ritsos**. The book I'm saving for summer to read is **Elena Ferrante**'s *My Brilliant Friend* and I'm still trying to read **Antonio Munoz Molina**'s *Sepharad*. Also for summer reading I have a copy of **Richard Flanagan**'s Booker Prize-winning *The Narrow Road to the Deep North* and, for teaching, I'm reading **Angela Carter**'s *The Bloody Chamber*, but of course I only teach books I want to read myself so it's never really a burden.

I don't think I can neglect my Kindle. As a married insomniac I plow through some books by the dim light of 4 a.m. until about 6 a.m. I'm finishing **Anthony Doerr**'s wonderful *All The Light We Cannot See* and looking forward to reading **Lily King**'s *Euphoria*. Books I don't feel I have to annotate usually make it into the Kindle.

I know it's more books than a person should be reading at any given time. Yet I have to have these books nearby. All of them. Even if I only scan a few pages. John Gardner, who was a teacher of mine, once said that writers don't read, they ravage. In a sense he gave me permission to do what I do anyway—scour books, newspapers, magazines for material. Everything becomes material. I don't really think of myself as the literary equivalent of Attila the Hun. I feel that I'm more like a hummingbird, dipping into dozens of flowers, sampling deep, then moving on.

Posted April 10, 2015

Valerie Nieman

Valerie Nieman's poems have appeared widely and been collected in her debut collection, *Wake Wake Wake*, and the new *Hotel Worthy,* as well as two chapbooks. She has held writing fellowships from the National Endowment for the Arts and the North Carolina Arts Council. Her books of prose include three novels, with the most recent, *Blood Clay*, being honored with the Eric Hoffer Award. She is a graduate of West Virginia University and Queens University of Charlotte. A professor of creative writing at North Carolina A&T State University, she teaches at John Campbell Folk School and other venues, and serves as poetry editor for *Prime Number Magazine*. You may encounter her on a train, or solo hiking, or over a cup of lemon-ginger tea at a local bookstore.

Read an excerpt from *Hotel Worthy* at wewantedtobewriters.com/arcology. Find out more about Valerie on her website, valnieman.com, or on Facebook at facebook.com/valerienieman1 and Twitter @valnieman.

José Saramago, *All the Names* — This book just left the bedside table (of which I am very fond, as I built it myself at John C. Campbell Folk School). This was my second venture into Saramago's wonderful parables that take place in the hearts of civil servants and lonely people who live on the fringe of their societies. I had read *Death With Interruptions* and was enchanted. In that novel, death decrees that no more people will die in this unnamed country, unleashing a cascade of events as people try to cope—until death takes human form and a new approach.

In *All the Names*, a low-level bureaucrat in the Central Registry of an unidentified city spends his days filling out birth and death forms with an antique pen and inkwell. In the evenings, in his poor little home attached to the side of the registry building, he obsesses over the lives of the famous and infamous in his country. But when he inadvertently collects the records of a young woman, his focus shifts to finding her. This new obsession takes him on strange nocturnal journeys both internal and external.

Saramago won the Nobel Prize in 1998, but his first attempt almost ended his writing career. According to *The Guardian*, he had sent out his first novel, *Skylight,* when he was 31 years old. It disappeared into the files of the publishing house, much the way things are mishandled and missing in the government bureaucracies he delineates. He did not write another novel for 20 years. He eventually returned to fiction and began publishing in the 1980s; in 1989, the publishers contacted him to say that the manuscript had been located in a move. He refused their offer of publication.

Ed Davis, *The Psalms of Israel Jones* — In the spirit of full disclosure, I received this book to blurb, and was absolutely delighted to do so. It's a great read, tracing the entwined lives of a fading rock and roll hero and his preacher son, complicated by past sins and the presence of apocalyptic cults. I found his depiction of people consumed by the spirit, whether of God or of music, to be true and compelling. Here's what I wrote: From the opening power chord to the feedback echoes that keep crashing through the mind after the last sentence, this novel is a rock testament to the power of music and the Word. Tight as a spring coiled to release and generous as an open hand, this is a book for fathers and sons, lovers, losers, doubters and believers—in short, for us all. *The Psalms of Israel Jones* was the 2010 Hackney Literary Award winner for the unpublished novel. Davis taught writing and humanities courses at Sinclair Community College in Dayton, Ohio, and at the Antioch Writers' Workshop.

Marc Hartzman, *American Sideshow* — Maybe not to everyone's taste for late-evening reading, if you are given to grotesque dreams. This is a compilation of short biographies and illustrations of sideshow "freaks" or naturals from the mid-19th century to the present. From the tamer curiosities of midgets and fat ladies to the truly bizarre—Turtle Boy, Alligator-Skinned Woman, the Human Torso, and the Man with Two Noses and Three Eyes—these are the stories of people who found their way in the world despite sometimes staggering odds. They sometimes made a lot of money, and more often than you might think, they found love.

Cheryl Strayed, *Wild* — You've probably seen the movie, and quite possibly read the book. I tend to fight shy of hugely popular products, but this book surprised me—not least because her story of traversing the wilderness to heal her wounded heart had real resonance for me. My mother died in September of 2012 from liver cancer, not a good end. Strayed's mother was also lost to cancer. She discovered healing while on the great solo walk of the Pacific Crest Trail. I headed for Scotland solo in 2014 with a 16-pound backpack—I was one up on her there, as she overloaded a huge backpack and suffered under that weight. Instead of carrying my home, I overnighted at B&Bs, inns, hostels (and once a tent) as I spent a month walking—across the country, then in Orkney, Iona, elsewhere. Not so great a feat as hers, but hey, I was 58 and had never done a through-hike in my life. So I felt echoes in her struggles to understand herself, her needs, and her grief—and the severe joys of time alone in the wild.

Cola Franzen, translator, *Poems of Arab Andalusia* — These poems were written at the height of Arab civilization in the Spanish peninsula, but remain as fresh today because of their direct approach and powerful sensuality. They are based on the 13th century codex of Ibn Sa'id, who sought poems "whose idea is more subtle than the West Wind, and whose language is more beautiful than a fair face." These are poems of a cultured warrior people, with verses that depict love and battle, sensual delights of wine and lovers, and the requirements of honor. A couple of excerpts:

From "My Beloved Comes":
*You came to me just before
the Christians rang their bells.
The half-moon was rising
looking like an old man's eyebrow
or a delicate instep.*

From "In the Battle":
*I saw her slim waist
among the lances
and when they leaned toward me
I embraced them.*

These mostly short poems had a strong influence on the Generation of '27 and especially Federico García Lorca, who was at work on a collection of poems inspired by Arabic forms when he was assassinated. I bought this book at City Lights in San Francisco (also the publisher) as a small reminder of the wonders of the Poetry Room.

Posted March 27, 2015

Cheryl Olsen

Cheryl Olsen is the web Goddess at wewantedtobewriters.com, responsible for securing/editing/formatting/proofing/posting all content. She also produces the site's monthly e-newsletter, the effervescent tweets at @2bwriters, and the lesser-loved posts at facebook.com/WeWantedToBeWriters. Learn more at wewantedtobewriters.com/our-authors/cheryl-olsen/.

For most of my life I've been a monogamous reader, faithfully consuming all the pages of one volume before perusing those of another. But the life of a book blogger, while long on books, tends to be short on the time to read them, and I am frequently forced into slutty relationships with multiple literary partners at a time. While initially appalled at this turn of fate, I have come to embrace it for several reasons:

- Reading two or four, sometimes even five books simultaneously encourages me to pay closer attention to all the elements of their respective genres, especially setting.
- It invites comparisons I might otherwise overlook.
- It tunes my ear to an author's language, diction, syntax in a way different from inhabiting one world at a time.

The ever-changing stack by my bed frequently includes advance review copies of recently or soon-to-be-released books. Let's start with a couple of historical novels, both with southern ties and racial themes:

Deborah Johnson, *The Secret of Magic* — This is based on the true story of a black soldier murdered on his way home to Mississippi at the end of WWII. An indefatigable Thurgood Marshall plays a part, but young black female Harlem attorney Reggie Robichard is the one who crosses the Mason-Dixon Line to confront the complicated racial conflicts and assumptions that propel the story. Shades of grey abound, few sexual, but all complex in the ways of generations of cultural intermingling. Everything about this compelling mystery seems authentic, including the titular book within a book.

Sarah McCoy, *The Mapmaker's Children* — McCoy interweaves the stories of two barren women, one a daughter of abolitionist John Brown, the other a present-day former advertising hotshot who's moved to rural West Virginia for a lower stress environment, and maybe to salvage her marriage. In many ways two separate novels in one, each with unique language, cadence, and temperament, it's the intertwining that lends weight and makes this more than a compelling set piece. McCoy has written other novels (*The Baker's Daughter*, *The Time It Snowed in Puerto Rico*), but I first encountered her in the *Grand Central* anthology. I hoped the writing would be as resonant this time around. I wasn't disappointed.

Kathie Giorgio, *Rise from the River* — I knew enough about this novel to brace for emotional and psychological turmoil, but I'd agreed to blurb it after reading her *Learning to Tell (A Life) Time*. Here's my blurb: The unthinkable is compounded by the unfathomable plunged in violence—guilt, lost faith, and silence seem inevitable. Yet in Kathie's capable hands, redemption is a reasonable expectation for the special family that is a young single mom, her four-year-old daughter, and their conservative landlady as they grapple with big questions. Though nothing comes easily in *Rise from the River*, light and love and healing permeate every gripping and satisfying page.

Polly Dugan, *The Sweetheart Deal* — Despite the double entendre, *The Sweetheart Deal* initially seemed too cavalier a title for the crushing sadness that opens and pervades Polly Dugan's debut novel. Expectations are high for the author of the stories that comprise last summer's well-received *So Much A Part of You* and this new work doesn't disappoint. Told from the alternating points of view of all the main players, Dugan explores the desolation of unexpected loss. The anger, numbness, and practical need to keep going for the sake of dependents ring true in crisp dialog and sharply realized characters. And thankfully, there's no quick fix for what ails Audrey and Garrett. So by the end, I accepted the title as a reward for the difficult journey to the light.

For somewhat lighter fare, I recommend three new volumes, two of which I'm still reading:

Tara Ison, *Reeling through Life: How I Learned to Live, Love and Die at the Movies* — I did say *somewhat* lighter. *Reeling through Life* is a collection of essays in the shape of a memoir that includes plenty of serious reflection on religion, family dynamics, alcoholism, and more along with a fine romp through dozens of major motion pictures and the lessons they imparted to Tara Ison at an impressionable, sometimes far too young age. It's a highly entertaining premise for a book, well written, and worthwhile if for no other reason than the nostalgic stroll through cinematic history. What were YOU doing when "One Flew Over the Cuckoo's Nest" and "The Graduate" hit the big screen? Were you even around?

Kim Korson, *I Don't Have a Happy Place: Cheerful Stories of Despondency and Gloom* — Another memoir, cloaked in snark and eliciting guffaws you'll be embarrassed to own up to. Jon Stewart says—right there on the front cover—"Kim Korson must be stopped. My wife thinks she's funnier than me." I'm still high-skipping through Barbie envy and the travails of sleep-away camp, but I'm pretty sure it's safe to say this will be the fullest half-empty glass you're likely to swig for a while.

Kathryn Leigh Scott, *Jinxed* — Kathryn's personal backstory is legendary—she played Josette DuPres, ingénue bride of reluctant vampire Barnabas Collins on the wildly popular TV cult classic "Dark Shadows," and is still a working actor with major street cred. So not surprisingly, *Jinxed* (released this month from Cumberland Press), a sequel to her *Down and Out* *in Beverly Heels*, draws heavily on that insider status. And to great effect. It's a mystery novel set in a Tinseltown only the cognoscenti usually get to see. Breezy without feeling fluffy, *Jinxed* continues the saga of an aging star who's about to be replaced in the role she created by an ambitious anti-ingénue who goes missing, leaving our heroine looking implicated. *Beverly Heels* tackled the plight of the formerly rich homeless in a town that's all about appearance. The sequel promises to go below the surface as well.

Posted February 20, 2015

Eric Olsen

Eric Olsen is the lead author of *We Wanted to Be Writers* and a regular contributor to this blog. Find out more at wewantedtobewriters.com.

A few weeks ago, a friend was thinning out the books on his shelves and stacked in corners in his living room and dining room and bedroom and even on the kitchen counter (he's a poet), and he invited me over to look at the books he was planning to get rid of, in case I might want one or two.

Or a dozen….

Of course I leapt at the chance to glom onto still more books, despite the fact I'm long, long overdue myself for a similar book-thinning. Among the books I grabbed and am reading now was:

William Goldman, *Adventures in the Screen Trade* — Goldman's the two-time Oscar-winning screenwriter and novelist. He wrote the screenplays for *Butch Cassidy and the Sundance Kid*, and *All the President's Men*, among many others, and the novel *Marathon Man*, and screenplay for the movie version.

The copy of *Adventures* that I got from my friend is a thick (594 pages) trade paperback, published in 1983. It was printed on cheap paper gone brown and brittle at the edges. I started reading it the night I got it; the front cover promptly fell off, and I've now been using it as a bookmark. But no matter…. It's a terrific read.

It's an "insider's" look at Hollywood, the business and people of filmmaking, and the art and craft of screenwriting, but an insider's look from the POV of an outsider. Or maybe it's an outsider's look from the inside. Whatever. Here's Goldman on his early impression of LA, not long after arriving from the outskirts of Chicago to work on *Butch*:

> Los Angeles terrifies me.
> But my particular crazies are not why I find writing so difficult. It's more this: Everything's so goddam *nice* out there.

I generally don't have a lot of patience with enormously successful guys writing about the awful burdens of their success, the burdens of their fabulous wealth and their fabulous fame and that fabulous house in Malibu overlooking the fabulous blue Pacific, but Goldman doesn't do much of it, and when he does, it's with a certain disarming wit.

Of more interest are his punchy, funny takes on the business of filmmaking. Here he is on studio executives:

> NOBODY KNOWS ANYTHING.
> Not one person in the entire motion picture field knows for a certainty what's going to work. Every time out it's a guess—and, if you're lucky, an educated one.

And here on *Raiders of the Lost Ark*:

> Raiders is the number-four film in history as this is being written. I don't remember any movie that had such power going in. It was more or less the brainchild of George Lucas and was directed by Steven Spielberg, the two unquestioned wunderkinder of show business (*Star Wars*, *Jaws*, etc.). Probably you knew that. But did you know that *Raiders of the Lost Ark* was offered to every single studio in town—
>
> > —*and they all turned it down?*
> > All except Paramount.
>
> Why did Paramount say yes? Because nobody knows anything. And why did all the other studios say no? Because nobody knows anything.

About half-way into the book, we get to the nuts-and-bolts stuff about script writing. This part includes the full script of *Butch Cassidy and the Sundance Kid*, plus Goldman's wry commentary on it. I'm not there yet, but am looking forward to it (I did sneak a peek and read a few pages last night). I'm always trying to write a screenplay. Maybe something of Goldman will rub off, or one can always hope…. If you're interested in movies, filmmaking, or script writing, or you just like a fun read, I highly recommend this book.

Robert Scheer, *They Know Everything About You: How Data-Collecting Corporations and Snooping Government Agencies Are Destroying Democracy* — If you're the sort who likes a nice little bout of raging paranoia before nodding off, then boy, this is the book for you.

I bought it about a month ago, after a lecture on privacy, or lack thereof, Scheer gave in Berkeley. Scheer's a professor at USC's Annenberg School for Communication (he also has an online magazine, truthdig.com—very interesting, check it out). Scheer's book is basically about how Google and Facebook and other such "private" internet firms are colluding with various government agencies such as the NSA, FBI, and local police to track our every move… and thought. Google and Facebook are invading our privacy because they're interested in selling us stuff; they're gathering every piece of information about us that they possibly can to anticipate what we want, and target ads accordingly. The government has other priorities, but the end result is the same, says Scheer, the destruction of our democracy.

Scheer argues that privacy *is* freedom (also the title of chapter four in the book), and that lack of privacy destroys democracy. The problem, Scheer says, is that we're happily tossing aside our privacy (and thus our freedom) for the sake of convenience as we buy stuff online (whenever you click that little "I agree" button below the pages of fine print none of us ever reads, you're agreeing to give up any expectation of privacy).

The Snowden revelations have forced companies such as Facebook and Google to make a show of fretting over our rights to privacy, but the fact is they continue to make available to the government all the information we give them, and all the other information about us they glom onto in other ways, such as our political views, which can be quite accurately assessed simply by noting the websites we click on.

Did someone say Orwell?

Indeed, the divide between corporations like Facebook and Google and government, police, and security agencies is more porous than ever—and that's the definition of fascism: a collusion of business, government, police, and military to control the people.

Scheer quotes Facebook founder Mark Zuckerberg trying to explain how this is no big deal, given the fact we give up our privacy quite willingly: "People have really gotten comfortable not only sharing more information and different kinds, but more openly and with more people. That social norm is just something that has evolved over time. We view it as our role in the system to constantly be innovating and be updating what our system is to reflect what the current social norms are."

So privacy's a "social norm," not a constitutionally guaranteed right?

Our founding fathers wrote the Fourth Amendment to the U.S. Constitution as a defense against the unlawful intrusions by tyrants into our privacy: "The right of the people to be secure in their persons, houses, papers, and effects, against unreasonable searches and seizures, shall not be violated...."

Apparently Zuckerberg skipped his civics class. And apparently Google's Eric Schmidt didn't get the memo, either. But of course profit always trumps ideals like democracy. Here's Schmidt on the topic: "If you have something that you don't want anyone to know, maybe you shouldn't be doing it in the first place." If anything, his attitude toward privacy is even more chilling.

Our founding fathers understood that the simple *fear* of intrusion was enough to stifle free speech, free assembly, and ultimately free thought, and that this fear is a choke-hold on democracy. Scheer's argument is that as a first step toward regaining our democracy, we need to start by being afraid again, very afraid. And then demanding a renewal of privacy protections at all levels, commercial and governmental.

I've just started Scheer's book (I paid cash for it—track *that*, NSA!), and until I finish Goldman's, I'll be reading Scheer in short spurts, usually when I need something depressing to read as a relief from Goldman's upbeat narrative.

Posted March 13, 2015

Judy Reeves

Judy Reeves is a writer, teacher, and writing practice provocateur who has written four books on writing, including *Wild Women, Wild Voices*, which was released in 2015, and the award-winning *A Writer's Book of Days*. Her work has appeared in magazines, literary journals, anthologies, and the textbook, *Expressive Writing: Classroom and Community*. She has edited several anthologies and chapbooks, including those born out of her Wild Women writing workshops, which she has led since 1997.

In addition to leading private writing groups, Judy teaches at University of California San Diego Extension and San Diego Writers, Ink, a nonprofit literary organization she cofounded. She also presents workshops at writing conferences and retreats internationally. Born in the Midwest, she has traveled throughout the world but somehow always finds her way back to San Diego, where she currently lives.

Read an excerpt from Judy's latest at wewantedtobewriters.com/arcology. Learn more about Judy on her website, judyreeveswriter.com.

One morning not long ago as I lay in savasana pose on my yoga mat and opened my eyes to all those loaded bookcases surrounding me, I had the eerie sense that "the Big One" (I live in California) could happen at any moment and I'd be crushed to death by books. Well, for a writer and a reader, I guess that's not the worst way to go, and even though mentioning it in light of the recent, deadly Kathmandu earthquake may be in bad taste, it tells me once again that I need to do some thinning. "Choose 100 of your favorites and let the rest go," I was advised. Easy for you to say.

Meantime, the books by my bed are a changing landscape. At least the ones at the top of the various stacks and piles. The ones at the bottom tend to gather dust, but I'm so sure I'm going to get to them "as soon as" that they stay and every once in a while, I unstack and rearrange them. In that stack: *Wolf Hall*, by **Hilary Mantel**. A friend who loved this book bought it for me at a used bookstore in Grover Beach, California, several years ago. Every time I open it and get past all the praise to the Cast of Characters and Family Tree, I get seized by intimidation and close it up again. (I've not seen the mini-series either.)

Another book, long in the stack of "next," but yet to be picked up, *The Book Thief* by **Markus Zusak**. I can't say why this one hasn't made it from beside the bed to in the bed yet, but just paging through it now, I'm tempted; it might be next. Except my friend and fellow writer **Andrew Roe**'s new book, *The Miracle Girl*, was just released. I went to Andy's reading at Warwick's Books to get my copy and can't wait to get inside. Eight-year-old Annabelle Vincent lies in a coma-like state, unable to move or speak, but because a visitor experienced what seemed like a miracle and believed it happened because of Annabelle, the crowds start coming. The sections Andy read were enticing and beautiful.

Later today I'm returning **Meg Wolitzer**'s *The Interestings* to the library. It's a hefty novel, 450-plus hardcover pages, which means I had to use a pillow to balance it while I read in bed. We meet the richly drawn cast of characters at a summer arts camp when they're young teens and travel with them, forward and backward, through middle age. The question—What is talent and what does it mean to have a little or a lot of it?—resonates with me. My own novel (fourth draft, still revising) asks the question "What is success?" and also begins in the teenage years of the protagonist. When I take Wolitzer's book back to the library today, I'm also taking my list of books to bring home that I'll place beside my bed. Unfortunately, *A Little Life* by **Hanya Yanagihara** has 33 holds on the library's 21 copies.

Other books that stay beside my bed for the occasional re-read or dive-into: **Terry Tempest Williams**' gorgeous book, *When Women Were Birds*, a meditation on mothers, women, nature, and history. This is a physically beautiful book, too, smallish, with French flaps and a title embossed in what resembles an old bookplate. **Diane Ackerman**'s *A Natural History of the Senses*, is also a perennial, but I keep it in the bookshelf near my desk where I prepare for classes. It's near the top of my list to recommend to my writing students. Every time I read or re-read a book by these writers, I consider myself a student.

I also consider myself a student of **Mary Oliver**. Current read: *Long Life: Essays and Other Writings*. Lyrical and wise and graceful, Oliver writes in a language that reaches deep inside. She tells of emerging from the woods on a sunny morning ("pouring-down sunlight") and is hit with a "*seizure* of happiness." I know that feeling; here writer and reader connect in a shared human experience—which may be the reason writers write and readers read: that exquisite connection.

And to remind myself of what matters, I read again and again, **Thomas Moore**'s *The Re-Enchantment of Everyday Life*. For me, more than his better known, *Care of the Soul*, this book serves as morning meditation and nighttime prayer.

Oh, and we haven't even talked about all the old, withering, dog-eared copies of the *New Yorker* that I swear I'll get to one of these naptimes or restless nights.

Posted May 15, 2015

Kathryn Leigh Scott

Kathryn Leigh Scott, author, publisher and actress is probably best known for her star turn as Josette DuPres, ingénue bride of reluctant vampire Barnabas Collins in the TV cult classic "Dark Shadows." Her third novel, *Jinxed: A Jinx Fogarty Mystery*, was released in early 2015. It is a sequel to her *Down and Out in Beverly Heels*. While continuing her acting career, Kathryn started Pomegranate Press to publish books about the entertainment industry, "Dark Shadows" and other companion books to classic TV series, and various nonfiction and fiction titles. She continues her acting career playing George Segal's girlfriend Miriam in "The Goldbergs" and appeared in the 2015 mid-season launch of "Marvel's Agents of S.H.I.E.L.D."

Read excerpt of *Jinxed* at wewantedtobewriters.com/arcology. Learn more about Kathryn and her work on her website, kathrynleighscott.com.

It's cold outside and snowing heavily, but this evening I'm tucked into my favorite chair with my feet up to begin reading **J.D. Horn**'s *The Source,* the third in his series of bewitching paranormal mysteries set in Savannah. I was captivated by *The Line*, which introduced Mercy and her family of witches, and couldn't wait for the first sequel, *The Void*.

In honor of **P.D. James**, I've plucked a couple of her books off my shelves to re-read, including *An Unsuitable Job for a Woman* and *A Certain Justice*. I have all her books and I treasure them. It's no secret that I love mysteries of a British persuasion and my bookshelves are crammed with the complete collections of Margery Allingham, Agatha Christie, Dorothy Sayers, and Josephine Tey, all comfortable classics I re-read and savor. I was an American living in London for many years; it's only now that I'm residing in New York that I'm setting my next mystery novel in England.

My bedside table also includes books by friends, including

Alan Russell's *Guardians of the Night*, another installment in his intriguing series featuring LAPD Detective Michael Gideon and his German Shepherd partner Sirius. For something completely different, I'm also reading *So, Anyway...* by my old friend **John Cleese**. I'm learning such a lot I didn't know about this insightful, scathingly funny, and very dear man.

Posted February 6, 2015

Nancy Slavin

Nancy Slavin is a long-time English literature, creative and composition writing instructor at the smallest community college in Oregon, as well as an educator for a non-profit working to end violence against women. Her novel, *Moorings*, was published in 2013, and more of her work can be found in *Rain Magazine*, *Barrelhouse*, *hip mama*, *Literary Mama*, *Oregon Humanities Magazine,* and *Chicago Literati*. Nancy has lived on the north Oregon coast for more than twenty years.

Learn more on her website, nancyslavin.com.

I finish almost every book I start. I read every word all the way to the end, even if it takes months, or, yes, years. For an English teacher, I'm a painfully slow reader who only perseveres because a professor once said, "What value is there in reading quickly?" Thus, there are several halfway-throughs in a pile next to my bed, because I'm reading several books at once. There are a few books in a pile on the bottom shelf of the table, which I have finished and they remain, like dust-covered sentinels guiding me.

Books on top that will be finished some day:

Azar Nafisi, *Reading Lolita in Tehran* — I know, I'm late to the party as usual. I love **Nabokov**, and have read many of his novels, but I hated *Lolita* (confession: I haven't finished it yet!) because I tried to read *Lolita* when I'd just started out as an educator regarding domestic and sexual violence. I could not get past the continual rape of the child. Thus, the title of Nafisi's book made me avoid it for years, but too many people told me to read it, so I am. Nafisi's explanations of how Western literature buoys her, her friends, and her students during the constant pressing down by militants in Iran are moving, and smart. Her story reminds me how literature connects us by leaving character motivations open-ended rather than absolute. As she says, "Our focus…is on the delicate spot where the prisoner touches the bar, on the invisible contact between flesh and cold metal," and as I read, I know freedom is a precarious abstraction, and literature keeps our minds free. Even though the memoir is ten years old, the story and Nafisi's writing is just as significant now as it was then. When I'm done with the memoir, I'll pick up *Lolita* again.

Thomas Hardy, *Tess of the D'Urbervilles* — An homage to my commitment to reading classic books I, a dilettante English major and instructor, have not yet read. I love Hardy's writing—"each was but portion of one organism called sex"—and the story of a girl's movement toward autonomy. I don't know why it's taking me so long to read. I do know I was struck with how artfully and compassionately Hardy deals with Alec's rape of Tess, especially in comparison to another book I picked up around the same time, **T. Coraghessan Boyle**'s *Drop City*, which is one of those books that will take me years to finish. I could be slow reading Hardy because I am enthralled with his use of language and with those days when good writing still mattered, a lot.

Diana Abu-Jaber, *Crescent* — Again, late to the party on this one, even though I've read three of her five books, *Arabian Jazz*, *The Language of Baklava,* and *Origins*, but haven't read *Crescent* yet. I'm only on Chapter Two and already, Abu-Jaber's juicy, sweet, and sensual writing shines through. Diana was my thesis advisor long ago at PSU, and she was kind, helpful, and a good reader, so I read her books.

The finished books on the bottom of the table:

David Vann, *Legend of a Suicide* — I met Mr. Vann at Wordstock in Portland a few years ago, because he read in a room with **Mary Rechner**, who'd just come out with *Nine Simple Patterns for Complicated Women* and I was a new mother and needed stories about being a mom. *Legend of a Suicide* is a compilation of stories, but the title story is why it remains near my bed. I can't say too much because I'll give too much away, but the story is about a father and a son and their complicated relationship, mostly brought on by the father's childish behavior and laying his burdens on his son. Let's just say the sins of the father are laid upon the child in a way that made me say, "Good lord, I did not see that coming," and left me breathless.

Sheila Nickerson, *Disappearance: A Map* — The subtitle is "A Meditation on Death and Loss in the High Latitudes." I'm writing a memoir about Alaska, so I read a lot of non-fiction set in Alaska. This book, which I stole from a friend's house, is a chronicle of people whose lives have been taken by Alaska, which the Great Land is bound to do. The log-like entry structure of this book is full of famous disappearances and contemporary ones, but the structure frustrated me because the log entries are a bit dull. Meanwhile, Nickerson's real story—the abuse in her childhood family, her leaving of a job—lurk in the shadows and never quite come to light. I finished *Disappearance* and really need to give my friend back her book.

Peggy Orenstein, *Cinderella Ate My Daughter* — As a feminist mother who, besides teaching and writing, has also worked for two decades as an educator for a non-profit organization seeking to end violence against women, the fact that my baby daughter morphed into a toddling Disneyfied princess was not only ironic, but extremely depressing. Orenstein's funny, personal, clear and critical analysis of how "Disney Princess" became a marketing strategy specifically geared toward younger and younger girls helped me to know I wasn't a complete feminist failure as a mom. She also warns me in that book of the hazards of teen years to come, and I'm terrified, so I keep the book by my bed like others keep a Bible.

Hermann Hesse, *Siddhartha*, translated by Sherab Chödzin Kohn — I'd never read it, always wanted to because I like to learn about people's spiritual awakenings, and reading the book, yes, took me a while. The plot, as we say, was slow, but

I was surprised by the way the main character—you know, Buddha—went through many machinations on his journey of self-awareness. He was less perfect than I might have thought, and he seemed not so different from me. The lesson is always the same; before enlightenment: chop wood, carry water. After enlightenment: chop wood, carry water. Keeps me humble.

Posted August 1, 2014

Therese Walsh

Therese Walsh is the author of two novels, *The Last Will of Moira Leahy* and her latest, *The Moon Sisters* (Crown, Random House) available in paperback and for Kindle and Nook. A self-professed foodie and amateur photographer, she's also the co-founder and editor-in-chief of Writer Unboxed, mother of two, and chief treat-giver to a Jack Russell Terrier.

Find out more at Therese's website, theresewalsh.com, or Writer Unboxed, writerunboxed.com.

I might be a book hoarder. I just want to get that out there, so we understand one another. I have so many books beside my bed, that if I tried to list them all, we'd be here for a long while. I would put you to sleep. You would wake again, your face tattooed with the imprint of the table you fell against or maybe a pattern of squares from your computer's keyboard. This would be unfortunate, and I do believe you'd resent me for it. Therefore, because I like to be liked, I'll tell you just a *few* of the books beside my bed. I'm going to share the first sentence of each of the profiled books here, too, because I think first sentences are important.

Kathryn Craft, *The Art of Falling* — Kathryn and I are online friends, meaning we got to know one another over Facebook. We had the opportunity to meet "IRL" (In Real Life) several months ago when she visited my local indie bookstore for a reading, and we bonded over dessert. It was a no-brainer that I pick up her novel. The novel is utterly compelling. First sentence: *My muscles still won't respond.* A mind-over-matter book, *The Art of Falling* is about a dancer's recovery of self, following an accident.

Leslye Walton, *The Strange and Beautiful Sorrows of Ava Lavender* — This one caught my eye several months back. I loved the simplicity of the cover, the gold feather; I loved the title. I don't know this author but I hear her talking my language via some of the descriptions in the flap copy. Words like *twins* and *dark* and *mute* and *mythology* make me purr, in a readerly way, and then there's this: The protagonist is born with bird wings. First sentence: *To many, I was myth incarnate, the embodiment of a most superb legend, a fairy tale.*

Katherine Howe, *Conversion* — I was fortunate enough to receive an Advance Reader Copy (ARC) of this novel, which was released July 1, 2014. I began reading it, then immediately set it aside. I knew as soon as I read the first graph that it would consume me, and I needed to wait until I had a clear weekend when it wouldn't matter if I shut down to the world. This is a YA novel about the second coming of witches in a Massachusetts high school. First graph: *How long must I wait?*

Nathan Filer, *Where the Moon Isn't* — Interestingly, though its title here in the states was *Where the Moon Isn't*, it appears to have been re-released under its UK title, *The Shock of the Fall*. Who knows why? It doesn't matter. This book is told from the perspective of a boy who is likely schizophrenic in the years following the loss of his brother. As an author who writes about loss, this one grabbed at me. Filer is a wordsmith and knows how to instill a work with Voice. I can appreciate already why he won the 2013 Costa Book of the Year. The first chapter, entitled "The Girl and Her Doll," starts with this sentence: *I should say that I am not a nice person.*

Jenny Milchman, *Cover of Snow* — This is my newest acquisition—a psychological thriller that is both character-rich and suspenseful, and that won the Mary Higgins Clark Award. The novel, Jenny's acclaimed debut, is the story of a woman in the wake of her husband's death. His apparent suicide takes on shades of conspiracy the deeper she digs for answers. The first sentence is a powerhouse: *My husband wasn't in bed with me when I woke up that January morning.*

Posted July 18, 2014

BOOKS BY OUR CONTRIBUTORS

Dale Bridges
Justice, Inc. (Monkey Puzzle Press, 2014)

David Corbett
The Mercy of the Night (Thomas & Mercer, 2015)
The Art of Character (Penguin, 2013)
The Devil's Redhead (Mysterious Press, 2012, reissue)
Do They Know I'm Running? (Ballantine, 2010)
Blood of Paradise (Ballantine, 2007)
Done for a Dime (Ballantine, 2004, reissue)

Lucille Lang Day
Becoming an Ancestor: Poems (Červená Barva Press, forthcoming 2015)
Dreaming of Sunflowers: Museum Poems (Blue Light Press, forthcoming 2015)
Married at Fourteen: A True Story (Heyday, 2012)
SEEK: Science Exploration, Excitement, and Knowledge (Children's Hospital Oakland, 2010)
The Curvature of Blue: Poems (Červená Barva Press, 2009)
God of the Jellyfish: Poems (Červená Barva Press, 2007
The Book of Answers: Poems (Finishing Line Press, 2006)
Chain Letter (Heyday, 2005)
Infinities: Poems (Cedar Hill Publications, 2002)
Lucille Lang Day: Greatest Hits 1975-2000 (Pudding House Publications, 2001)
Wild One: Poems (Scarlet Tanager Books, 2000)
Fire in the Garden: Poems (Mother's Hen Press, 1997)
Self-Portrait with Hand Microscope: Poems (Berkeley Poets Workshop and Press, 1982)
How to Encourage Girls in Math and Science (Prentice-Hall, 1982)

Polly Dugan
The Sweetheart Deal (Little, Brown and Company, 2015) and *So Much a Part of You* (Little, Brown and Company, 2014)

Grant Faulkner
Fissures: One Hundred 100-Word Stories (Press 53, 2015)

Wendy Fox
Deals (forthcoming from Underground Voices, 2016)
The Seven Stages of Anger and Other Stories (Press 53, 2014)

Clifford Garstang
Everywhere Stories: Short Fiction from a Small Planet, editor (Press 53, 2014)
What the Zhang Boys Know (Press 53, 2012)
In an Uncharted Country (Press 53, 2009)

Kathie Giorgio
Rise From The River (Main Street Rag, 2015)
Learning To Tell (A Life)Time (Main Street Rag, 2013)
Enlarged Hearts (Main Street Rag, 2012)
The Home For Wayward Clocks (Main Street Rag, 2011)

Kate Gray
Carry the Sky (Forest Avenue Press, 2014)
Another Sunset We Survive (Cedar House Books, 2007)
Bone-Knowing (Gertrude Press, 2006),
Where She Goes (Blue Light Press, 2000)

Therése Halscheid
Frozen Latitudes (Press 53, 2014)
Uncommon Geography (Carpenter Gothic, 2006)
Without Home (Kells Media Group, 2001)

Powertalk (Therese Halscheid, 1995)

Tara Ison
Reeling Through Life: How I Learned to Live, Love, and Die at the Movies (Soft Skull Press, 2015)
Rockaway: A Novel (Soft Skull Press, 2013)
A Child Out of Alcatraz (Forever Press, 2012)
The List: A Novel (Scribner, 2011, reprint edition)

Pam Jenoff
The Last Summer at Chelsea Beach (Harlequin MIRA, 2015)
The Winter Guest (Harlequin MIRA, 2014)
The Other Girl (Harlequin MIRA, 2014)
The Ambassador's Daughter (Harlequin MIRA, 2013)
The Things We Cherished (Anchor, 2012, reprint edition)
A Hidden Affair (Atria, 2010)
Almost Home (Atria, 2009)
The Diplomat's Wife (Harlequin MIRA, 2008)
The Kommandant's Girl (Harlequin MIRA, 2007)

Nicole C. Kear
Now I See You (St. Martin's Press, 2014)

Kim Korson
I Don't Have a Happy Place: Cheerful Stories of Despondency and Gloom (Gallery Books, 2015)

April Lindner
Catherine (Poppy, 2015))
Jane (Poppy, 2010)
Love, Lucy (Poppy, 2015)
Skin (Texas Tech University Press, 2002)
This Bed Our Bodies Shaped (Able Muse Press, 2012)
Contemporary American Poetry, co-editor with R.S. Gwynn (Longman, 2004)

Lineas Conectadas, editor with Hernan Lara Zavala, translator (Sarabande 2006)

Jonnie Martin
Wrangle (CreateSpace, 2014)

Felicia Mitchell
Waltzing with Horses (Press 53, 2014)
The Cleft of the Rock (Finishing Line Press, 2009)
Her Words: Diverse Voices in Contemporary Appalachian Women's Poetry (University of Tennessee, 2002)

Mary Morris
The Jazz Palace (Nan A. Talese/Doubleday, 2015)
The River Queen (Holt, 2007)
The Virago Illustrated Book of Women Writers (Virago UK, 2007)
Revenge (Picador, 2004)
Acts of God (Picador, 2001)
Angels & Aliens (Picador, 1999)
The Lifeguard (Nan A. Talese/Doubleday, 1998)
House Arrest (Nan A. Talese/Doubleday, 1998)
*A Mother's Love (*Nan A. Talese/Doubleday, 1997)
Maiden Voyages: Writings of Women Travelers (Vintage, 1993)
Wall to Wall: From Beijing to Berlin by Rail (Nan A. Talese/Doubleday Books, 1992)
The Waiting Room (Doubleday, 1989)
Nothing to Declare: Memoirs of a Woman Traveling Alone (Houghton Mifflin Harcourt, 1988)
The Bus of Dreams: Stories (Houghton Mifflin, 1985)

Valerie Nieman
Hotel Worthy (Press 53, 2015)
Neena Gathering (a Post-Apocalyptic Novel) (Permuted Press, 2013; first edition Pageant Books, 1988)

Blood Clay (Press 53, 2011)
Wake Wake Wake (Press 53, 2006)
Fidelities (Vandalia Press, 2004)
Survivors (Van Neste Books, 2000)
How We Live (State Street Press chapbooks, 1996)

Eric Olsen
We Wanted to be Writers: Life, Love, and Literature in the Iowa Writers' Workshop (Skyhorse, 2011)

Judy Reeves
Wild Women, Wild Voices: Writing from Your Authentic Wildness (New World Library, 2015)
A Writer's Book of Days: A Spirited Companion and Lively Muse for the Writing Life (New World Library, 2010, revised edition)
The Writer's Retreat Kit: A Guide for Creative Exploration and Personal Expression (New World Library, 2005)
A Creative Writer's Kit: A Spirited Companion and Lively Muse for the Writing Life (New World Library, 2003)
Writing Alone, Writing Together: A Guide for Writers and Writing Groups (New World Library, 2002)

Kathryn Leigh Scott
Jinxed: A Jinx Fogarty Mystery (Cumberland Press, 2015)
Down and Out in Beverly Heels (Montlake Romance, 2013)
Dark Passages (Pomegranate Press, 2011)
Dark Shadows: Return to Collinwood (Pomegranate, 2011)
Dark Shadows Memories (2006)
The Bunny Years (Pomegranate, 1998)

Nancy Slavin
Oregon Pacific (Bay City Books, 2015)
Moorings (Feather Mountain Press, 2013)

Therese Walsh
The Moon Sisters (Crown, Random House, 2014)
The Last Will of Moira Leahy: A Novel (Broadway Books, 2010)

BOOKS DISCUSSED

FICTION
Including novels, short stories, drama, anthologies, young adult, and graphic novels

A

Diana Abu-Jaber, *Origins* (W.W. Norton, 2008, reprint edition); *Crescent* (W.W. Norton & Co., 2003); and *Arabian Jazz* (W.W. Norton, 2003), all 92

Aeschylus, 39

Louisa May Alcott, *Little Women* (Roberts Brothers, 1868-9), 66

Nelson Algren, *The Man with the Golden Arm* (Seven Stories Press, 1986), 26

Steve Almond and **Julianna Baggott**, *Which Brings Me to You: A Novel in Confessions* (Algonquin Books, 2006), 16

Aristophanes, 39

Jami Attenberg, *The Middlesteins* (Grand Central Publishing, 2012), 16

Margaret Atwood, *The Blind Assassin: A Novel* (Anchor, 2001); *The Handmaid's Tale* (Anchor, 1998); *Cat's Eye* (Anchor, 1998); *The Robber Bride* (Anchor, 1998); and *Alias Grace* (Anchor, 1997, reprint edition), all 40

B

Paolo Bacigalupi, *The Windup Girl* (Nightshade Books, 2009), 67

Lisa Barr, *Fugitive Colors* (Arcade Publishing, 2015), 49

Roland Barthes, *A Lover's Discourse: Fragments* (Hill

and Wang, 2010), 19

Karen Bender, *Refund: Stories* (Counterpoint, 2015), 47

Wendell Berry, *A Place on Earth* (Counterpoint, 2001), 64

Lee Blessing, *Eleemosynary* (Dramatists Play Service, 1998), 39

Amy Bloom, *Lucky Us* (Random House, 2014), 49

Chris Bohjalian, *Close Your Eyes, Hold Hands* (Vintage, 2015, reprint edition), 49

T. Coraghessan Boyle, *Drop City* (Penguin Books, 2004, reprint edition), 92

Ray Bradbury, *Fahrenheit 451* (Simon & Schuster, 2013, reprint edition), 38; *The Martian Chronicles* (Simon & Schuster, 2012, reprint edition); *The Illustrated Man* (Simon & Schuster, 2012, reprint edition); and *Something Wicked This Way Comes* (Avon, 2006, reprint edition), 39

Hermann Broch, *The Sleepwalkers* (Vintage, 1996), 20

Polly Buckingham, *A Year of Silence* (University of Central Florida College of Arts & Humanities, English Department, 1914), 22

C

Meg Cabot, *The Princess Diaries* (HarperTeen, 2000), 66

Italo Calvino, *Italian Folktales* (Mariner Books, 1992, reissue edition), 53

Jacqueline Carey, *Kushiel's Dart* (Tor Fantasy, 2002), 65

Angela Carter, *The Bloody Chamber* (Penguin Classics, 2015), 72

Maud Casey, *The Man Who Walked Away* (Bloomsbury, 2014), 27

Michael Chabon, *Telegraph Avenue* (HarperCollins 2012); *The Amazing Adventures of Kavalier & Clay* (Random House, 2009), both 66

John Cheever, *The Stories of John Cheever* (Ballantine, 1980), 14

Stuart Archer Cohen, *This Is How it Really Sounds* (St. Martin's Press, 2015), 8

Kathryn Craft, *The Art of Falling* (Sourcebooks Landmark, 2014), 95

Justin Cronin, *Mary and O'Neil: a Novel in Stories* (Dial Press, 2002), 15

D

Roald Dahl, *Kiss Kiss* (Penguin Books, 2011), 39

Ed Davis, *The Psalms of Israel Jones* (West Virginia University Press, 2014), 74

Sarah Dessen, *This Lullaby* (Viking Children's Books, 2002), 65

Anita Diamant, *The Red Tent* (Picador, 2010, 10th anniversary edition), 40

Anthony Doerr, *All the Light We Cannot See* (Scribner, 2014), 32 & 72

Ivan Doig, *Dancing at the Rascal Fair* (Scribner, 1996, reprint edition), 61

Fyodor Dostoevsky, *Notes from the Underground* (Vintage, 1984, reprint edition), 44

Brian Doyle, *Mink River* (Oregon Stage University Press, 2010), 63

Polly Dugan, *The Sweetheart Deal* (Little, Brown and Company, 2015); *So Much a Part of You* (Little, Brown and Company, 2014), both 78

E

Okla Elliott, *From the Crooked Timber* (Press 53, 2011), 5

Euripides, 39

F

William Faulkner, *Intruder in the Dust* (Vintage, 1991); *As I Lay Dying* (Vintage, 1991), both 63

Elena Ferrante, *My Brilliant Friend* (Europa Editions, 2012), 72

Helen Fielding, *Bridget Jones's Diary*, 40

Julia Fierro, *Cutting Teeth* (St. Martin's Press, 2014), 51

Nathan Filer, *Where the Moon Isn't* (St. Martin's Press, 2013), 96

F. Scott Fitzgerald, *The Great Gatsby* (Scribner, 2004), 38; *Tender is the Night* (Scribner, 1995, reprint edition), 19

Richard Flanagan, *The Narrow Road to the Deep North* (Vintage, 2015), 72

E. M. Forster, *A Passage to India* (Penguin Classics, 2011), 59

Karen Joy Fowler, *We Are All Completely Beside Ourselves* (Plume, 2014), 52

G

James Galvin, *Fencing the Sky* (Picador, 2000), 62

Kathie Giorgio, *Rise From The River* (Main Street Rag,

2015); *Learning To Tell (A Life)Time* (Main Street Rag, 2013), both 78

Molly Gloss, *The Jump-Off Creek* (Mariner Books, 2005, reprint edition), 61

Tod Goldberg, *Gangsterland* (Counterpoint, 2014), 47

Lady Augusta Gregory, with an introduction by William Butler Yeats, *Gods and Fighting Men* (in the public domain), 7

Susan Gubernat, editor, *Arroyo Literary Review* (California State University, East Bay, Spring 2014), 11

Heather Gudenkauf, *Little Mercies* (Harlequin MIRA, 2014), 49

Stephen D. Gutierrez, *The Mexican Man in His Backyard: Stories & Essays* (Roan Press, 2014), 12

H

Kristen Hannah, introduction, *Grand Central: Original Postwar Stories of Love and Reunion* (Berkley, 2014), 49, 78

Thomas Hardy, *Tess of the D'Urbervilles* (Penguin Classics edition, 2009), 92

Kent Haruf, *Plainsong* (Vintage, 2000), 62

Nathaniel Hawthorne, 39

Ursula Hegi, *Stones From the River* (Simon & Schuster, 1995), 39

Hermann Hesse, *Siddhartha*, translated by Sherab Chödzin Kohn (Shambala Publications, 2000), 93

J.D. Horn, *The Source: A Witching Savannah Novel* (47North, 2014); *The Void: A Witching Savannah Novel* (47North, 2014), both 89

Katherine Howe, *Conversion* (Speak, 2015, reprint edition), 96

Helen Humphreys, *Coventry: a Novel* (W.W. Norton, 2010); *Wild Dogs: a Novel* (W.W. Norton, 2006, reprint edition); *The Lost Garden: a Novel* (W.W. Norton, 2003, reprint edition); *Afterimage* (HarperCollins Canada, 2001), all 47

J

P.D. James, *A Certain Justice* (Ballantine books, 2003, reissue); *An Unsuitable Job for a Woman* (Touchstone, 2001), both 89

Adam Johnson, *The Orphan Master's Son* (Random House 2012), 27

Deborah Johnson, *The Secret of Magic* (Berkley Books, 2014), 77

Denis Johnson, *Train Dreams* (Picador, 2012), 62

James Joyce, *Ulysses* (Sylvia Beach, 1922), 66

Elise Juska, *The Blessings* (Grand Central Publishing, 2014), 15

K

Elizabeth Kadetsky, *The Poison that Purifies You* (C&R Press, 2014), 27

John Keeble, *The Shadows of Owls* (University of Washington Press, 2013), 23

Lily King, *Euphoria* (Grove Press, 2015), 72

Stephen King, *The Shining* (Anchor, 2012, reprint edition); *The Stand* (Anchor, 2012, reprint edition); *The Dead Zone* (Signet, 1980, reissue edition), all 38

Barbara Kingsolver, *Flight Behavior* (HarperCollins, 2013), 70

Ella Korson, *Don't Ask Me How it Happened* (in the works), 56

Mary Kubica, *The Good Girl* (Mira, 2015, reprint edition), 49

L

Wally Lamb, *I know This Much Is True* (Harper Perennial, 2008), 40; *She's Come Undone* (Pocket Books, 1998), 39

Harper Lee, *To Kill a Mockingbird* (Harper Perennial, 2002), 41

Dennis Lehane, *World Gone By* (William Morrow, 2015), 7

Madeleine L'Engle, *A Wrinkle in Time* (Square Fish, reprint edition, 2007), 51

Gail Carson Levine, *Ella Enchanted* (HarperCollins, 1997), 66

David Levithan, *Every Day* (Ember, 2013), 57

Henry Wadsworth Longfellow, 39

M

Susan Elia MacNeal, *The Prime Minister's Secret Agent* (Bantam, 2014), 48

Hilary Mantel, *Bring Up The Bodies* (Picador, 2013, reprint edition), 46; *Wolf Hall* (Fourth Estate, 2009), 34, 87

Peter Matthiesen, *Far Tortuga* (Vintage, 1988), 21

Cormac McCarthy, *Border Trilogy* (Everyman's Library, 1999), 62

Sarah McCoy, *The Mapmaker's Children* (Crown, 2015), 78; *The Baker's Daughter* (Broadway Books, 2012, reprint edition), 49, 78; *The Time it Snowed in Puerto Rico*

(Broadway Books, 2010, reprint edition), 78

Ron McLarty, *The Dropper* (Cemetery Dance Publications, 2012); *Art In America* (Penguin Books, 2009, reprint edition); *Traveler* (Penguin Books, 2008, reprint edition); *The Memory of Running* (Penguin, 2005), all 30

Jenny Milchman, *Cover of Snow* (Ballantine Books, 2013), 96

C. Talmadge Mitchell, *Dark Sings a Distant Herald: A Christmas Story on Holding Back the British Twilight* (Kindle Edition, 2014), 69

Antonio Munoz Molina, *Sepharad* (Harvest Books, 2008), 72

Toni Morrison, *Beloved* (Vintage, 2004, reprint edition); *Jazz* (Vintage, 2004, reprint edition), both 40

N

Celeste Ng, *Everything I Never Told You* (Penguin Books, 2015), 54

Vladimir Nabokov, *Lolita* (Vintage reiusse, 1989), 91

O

Jenny Offill, *Dept. of Speculation* (Vintage, 2014), 21

P

Dorothy Parker, *Complete Stories* (Penguin Classics, 2002), 41

Ann Patchett, *State of Wonder* (HarperCollins, 2011), 70; *Bel Canto* (Harper Perennial, 2008, reissue edition), 40

Tom Perrotta, *Bad Haircut: Stories From the Seventies* (St. Martin's Griffin, 2012, reprint edition), 55

Tamora Pierce, *Song of the Lioness Quartet* (first book,

Alanna: The First Adventure in the series published in 1983 by Atheneum (now part of Simon & Schuster), 65

Sylvia Plath, *The Bell Jar* (Harper Perennial Modern Classics, 2013), 38

E. Annie Proulx, *The Shipping News* (Scribner, 1994), 41

Marcel Proust, 20

Q

Anna Quindlen, *One True Thing* (Random House, 2006); *Black and Blue* (Random House, 2010), both 40

R

Midge Raymond, *Forgetting English* (Press 53, 2011), 22

Mary Rechner, *Nine Simple Patterns for Complicated Women* (Propeller Books, 2010), 92

Stacy Richter, *Twin Study* (Counterpoint, 2007), 5

Andrew Roe, *The Miracle Girl* (Algonquin Books, 2015), 87

Judith Rossner, *Looking For Mr. Goodbar* (Simon & Schuster, 2014, reissue); *Attachments* (Simon & Schuster, 2014, Kindle edition); *Emmeline* (Simon & Schuster, 2014, Kindle edition), all 38

Rainbow Rowell, *Eleanor and Park* (St. Martin's Griffin, 2013), 52

Anuradha Roy, *The Folded Earth* (Free Press, 2012), 70

Alan Russell, *Guardians of the Night* (Thomas & Mercer, 2015), 90

S

J.D. Salinger, *The Catcher in the Rye* (Little, Brown and Company, 1991), 38 & 40

James Salter, *Light Years* (Vintage, 1995, reissue edition), 21

José Saramago, *Death With Interruptions* (Mariner Books, reprint edition, 2009); *All the Names* (Harcourt, Inc. 2001); both 73

Kathryn Leigh Scott, *Jinxed: A Jinx Fogarty Mystery* (Cumberland Press, 2015); *Down and Out in Beverly Heels* (Montlake Romance, 2013), both 79

Taiye Selasi, *Ghana Must Go* (Penguin Books, 2013), 67

Maria Semple, *Where'd You Go, Bernadette* (Back Bay Books, 2013, reprint edition), 55

Shakespeare, 39

Sharma Shields, *The Sasquatch Hunter's Almanac* (Holt Paperbacks, 2015), 55

Carter Sickels, The *Evening Hour* (Bloomsbury USA, 2012), 36

Jon Skovron, *Man Made Boy* (Viking Books for Young Readers, 2013), 59

Nancy Slavin, *Moorings* (Feather Mountain Press, 2013), 36

Jane Smiley, *The Greenlanders* (Anchor, 2005, reprint edition); *A Thousand Acres* (Anchor, 2003, reprint edition), both 40

Lee Smith, *Guests on Earth* (Shannon Ravenel, 2013), 70

Zadie Smith, *NW* (Hamish Hamilton, 2014); *On Beauty* (Hamish Hamilton, 2005); *The Autograph Man* (Hamish

Hamilton, 2002); *White Teeth* (Hamish Hamilton, 2000), all 66

Sophocles, 39

Gregory Spatz, *Inukshuk* (Bellevue Literary Press, 2012), 23

Wallace Stegner, *Angle of Repose* (Vintage, 2014, reprint edition), 61

T

Donna Tartt, *The Goldfinch* (Back Bay Books, 2015), 59, 68; *The Secret History* (Vintage, 2004), 39

Jim Thompson, *Savage Night* (Vintage, reprint edition, 1991), 5

Ted Thompson, *The Land of Steady Habits* (Little, Brown and Company, 2014), 14

Paul Torday, *Salmon Fishing In The Yemen* (Mariner Books, 2008), 29

Barbara Trapido, *Brother of the More Famous Jack* (Bloomsbury USA, 2014), 55

Jonathan Tropper, *This Is Where I Leave You* (Plume, reprint edition, 2010), 16 & 56

Anne Tyler, *A Spool of Blue Thread* (Knopf, 2015), 29; *The Beginner's Goodbye* (Knopf, 2012), 70; *The Clock Winder* (Ballantine Books, 1996, reissue edition), 29

V

David Vann, *Legend of a Suicide* (Harper Perennial, 2010), 92

Kurt Vonnegut, *Slaughterhouse-Five* (Dell, 1991), 39

Susan Vreeland, *Lisette's List* (Random House, 2014), 49

W

Alice Walker, *The Temple of My Familiar* (Mariner Books, 2010, reprint edition); *Possessing the Secret of Joy* (The New Press, 2008); *The Color Purple* (Mariner Books, 2003), all 40

David Foster Wallace, *Infinite Jest* (Little, Brown, 1996), 20, 67

Michael Wallner, *April in Paris* (Anchor, 2008, reprint edition), 58

Leslye Walton, *The Strange and Beautiful Sorrows of Ava Lavender* (Candlewick, 2015), 95

Josh Weil, *The Great Glass Sea* (Grove, 2014), 25

Jennifer Weiner, *Good in Bed* (Washington Square Press, 2002, reprint edition), 40

Jincy Willett, *Amy Falls Down* (Picador, 2014), 4

Jacqueline Wilson, *Girls Under Pressure* (Doubleday, 1998), 65

Jeanette Winterson, *The Passion* (Grove Press, 1997), 39

Meg Wolitzer, *The Interestings* (Riverhead Books, 2013), 87

Virginia Woolf, *The Waves* (Harvest Books, 1978), 21; *Mrs. Dalloway* (Hogarth Press, 1925), 66

Austin Wright, *Tony and Susan* (Grand Central Publishing, 2011 reissue; originally published in 1993), 6

Y

Hanya Yanagihara, *A Little Life* (Doubleday, 2015), 87

Tiphanie Yanique, *Land of Love and Drowning* (Riverhead Books, 2014), 67

Z

Markus Zusak, *The Book Thief* (Knopf, 2005), 87

POETRY
Including translations and anthologies

A

W.H. Auden, *Collected Poems* (Vintage, 1991, reprint edition), 41

B

John Berryman, *Dream Songs* (Farrar, Straus and Giroux, 2014, reprint edition), 19

C

Angela Carter, *Memory Chose a Woman's Body* (Unbound Content, 2014), 26

Cameron Conaway, *Until You Make the Shore* (Salmon Poetry, 2014), 27

ee cummings, *Selected Poems 1923-1958* (Faber & Faber Poetry, 1977), 38 & 41

F

Cola Franzen, translator, *Poems of Arab Andalusia* (City Lights Books, 1989), 75

G

Louise Gluck, *Wild Iris* (Ecco, 1993, reprint edition), 43

H

Homer, *The Odyssey* (Penguin Classics, 1999, reprint edition); *The Iliad* (Penguin Classics, 1998, reprint edition), both 39

L

Daniel J. Langton, *Personal Effects: New and Selected Poems* (Blue Light Press/1st World Publishing, 2014), 11

N

Pablo Neruda, *Twenty Love Poems and a Song of Despair* (Chronicle Books, 1993), 38; *Full Woman, Fleshly Apple, Hot Moon: Selected Poems* (Harper Perennial, 2009), 58

O

Frank O'Hara, *Lunch Poems* (City Lights Publishers, 2001), 19

Alicia Suskin Ostriker, *The Old Woman, the Tulip, and the Dog* (University of Pittsburgh Press, 2014), 13

P

Dorothy Parker, *Complete Poems* (Penguin Classics, 2010), 41

R

Yannis Ritsos, *Diaries of Exile* (Archipelago, 2013), 72

Rumi, *The Essential Rumi*, translated by Coleman Barks with John Moyne (HarperSanFrancisco, 1995), 69

Leslie M. Rupracht, *Splintered Memories* (Main Street Rag, 2015), 30

S

Wislawa Szymborska, *People on a Bridge* (Forest Books, 1990); *View With a Grain of Sand* (Harcourt Brace, 1995), both 40

W

Walt Whitman, *Leaves of Grass* (Penguin Classics, 2003), 38, 39, & 41

NONFICTION
Including histories, biographies, essays, memoirs, and anthologies

A

Diana Abu-Jaber, *The Language of Baklava* (Anchor, 2006), 92

Diane Ackerman, *A Natural History of Love* (Vintage, 1995), 40 & 88

Eben Alexander, *Proof of Heaven: a Neurosurgeon's Journey into the Afterlife* (Simon & Schuster, 2013), 70

Aristotle, 39

A.J. Ayer, *The Problem of Knowledge* (St. Martin's Press, 1958), 26

B

Blake Bailey, *Cheever: A Life* (Vintage, 2010, reprint edition), 20

Alison Bechdel, *Fun Home: A Family Tragicomic* (Mariner Books, 2007, reprint edition), 55

Stanley L. Bentley, *Native Orchids of the Southern Appalachian Mountains* (UNC Press, 2000), 69

Birds Illustrated by Color Photography 1897 (Nature Study Publishing Company), 70

Harold Bloom, *Shakespeare: The Invention of the Human* (Riverhead Books, 1998), 33

Judy Blunt, *Breaking Clean* (Vintage, 2003, reprint edition), 63

Benjamin Busch, *Dust to Dust* (Norton, 2012), 26

C

Joseph Campbell, *The Power of Myth* (Anchor, 1991),

39 & 41

James Carroll, *Jerusalem, Jerusalem: How the Ancient City Ignited Our Modern World* (Houghton Mifflin Harcourt, 2011), 33

John Cleese, *So, Anyway…* (Crown Archetype, 2014), 90

Christopher Columbus, *The Diaries of Christopher Columbus*, 72

Deborah Morris Coryell, *Good Grief: Healing through the Shadow of Loss* (Healing Arts Press, 2007), 70

Peter Coyote, The Rainman's Third Cure (Counterpoint, 2015), 19

D

John D'Agata, editor, *The Next American Essay* (Graywolf Press, 2003), 44

Patricia Damery and **Naomi Ruth Lowinsky**, editors, *Marked by Fire: Stories of the Jungian Way* (Fisher King Press, 2012), 10

Marlena De Blasi, *A Thousand Days in Venice: an Unexpected Romance* (Algonquin Books, 2013, reprint edition); *A Thousand Days in Tuscany: a Bittersweet Adventure* (Ballantine Books, 2005, reprint edition), both 59

Joan Didion, *The Year of Magical Thinking* (vintage, 2007, reprint edition), 44

Annie Dillard, *Pilgrim at Tinker Creek* (Harper Perennial, 2013), 44

Andre Dubus III, *Townie: a Memoir* (W.W. Norton, 2012, reprint edition), 45

E

Ralph Waldo Emerson, 39

G

James Galvin, *The Meadow* (Holt Paperbacks, 1993, reprint edition), 61

Roxane Gay, *Bad Feminist: Essays* (Harper Perennial, 2014), 67

William Goldman, *Adventures in the Screen Trade* (Warner Books, 1983), 81

Lucy Grealy, *Autobiography of a Face* (Harper Perennial, 2003), 40 & 45

H

Carl Hart, *High Price* (Harper, 2013), 27

Marc Hartzman, *American Sideshow* (Jeremy P. Tarcher/Penguin, 2005), 74

Ernest Hemingway, *A Moveable Feast* (Scribner reprint edition, 2010), 42

Lewis Hyde, *The Gift: Creativity and the Artist in the Modern World* (Vintage, 2007), 20

I

Tara Ison, *Reeling Through Life: How I Learned to Live, Love, and Die at the Movies* (Soft Skull Press, 2015), 79

K

Elizabeth Kolbert, *The Sixth Extinction* (Henry Holt, 2014), 25

Kim Korson, *I Don't Have a Happy Place: Cheerful Stories of Despondency and Gloom* (Gallery Books, 2015), 79

L

Anne Lamott, *Small Victories: Spotting Improbably Moments of Grace* (Riverhead Books, 2014), 41; *Traveling*

Mercies: Some Thoughts on Faith (Anchor, 2000), 40

Dinah Lenney, *The Object Parade* (Counterpoint, 2015), 47

Jill Leovy, *Ghettoside: A True Story of Murder in America* (Spiegel & Grau, 2015), 8

M

Lee Martin, *From Our House: a Memoir* (Bison Books, 2009), 45

Domingo Martinez, *The Boy Kings of Texas* (Lyons Press, 2012), 63

Barbara Medina and **Victor Medina**, *Central Appalachian Wildflowers* (Falcon, 2002), 69

Rosa Montero, *Pasiones* (Punto de Lectura, 1999), 33

Rick Moody, *On Celestial Music: And Other Adventures in Listening* (Back Bay Books, 2012), 72

Thomas Moore *The Re-Enchantment of Everyday Life* (Harper Collins, 1996); *Care of the Soul* (Harper Collins, 1992), both 88

N

Azar Nafisi, *Reading Lolita in Tehran* (Random House, 2004), 91

Maggie Nelson, *Bluets* (Wave Books, 2009), 72

Royal Case Nemiah, *Selections from Ancient Greek Historians in English* (Charles Scribners & Sons, 1939), 7

Sheila Nickerson, *Disappearance: A Map* (Harvest Books, 1996), 93

O

Mary Oliver, *Long Life — Essays and Other Writings* (De Capo Press, 2005), 88

Peggy Orenstein, *Cinderella Ate My Daughter: Dispatches from the Front Lines of the New Girlie-Girl Culture* (HarperCollins, 2011), 93

P

Ann Patchett, *Truth & Beauty: A Friendship* (Harper Perennial, 2005, reprint edition), 40 & 45

R

Claudia Rankine, *Citizen: An American Lyric* (Graywolf Press, 2014), 72

Matt Ridley, *Genome: the Autobiography of a Species in 23 Chapters* (Harper Perennial, 2001), 70

Mark Rotella, *Stolen Figs and Other Adventures in Calabria* (North Point Press, 2004), 58

S

Oliver Sacks, *Hallucinations* (Knopf, 2012), 70

Sharon Salzberg, *Loving-Kindness: The Revolutionary Art of Happiness* (Shambala, 1995), 33

Andrea Maloney Schar, *Your Mindful Compass: Breakthrough Strategies for Navigating Life/Work Relationships in Any Social Jungle* (Ideas to Action, 2013), 69

Robert Scheer, *They Know Everything About You: How Data-Collecting Corporations and Snooping Government Agencies Are Destroying Democracy* (Nation Books, 2015), 83

Dan Silverman and **Idelle Davidson**, *Your Brain After Chemo: A Practical Guide to Lifting the Fog and Getting Back Your Focus* (Da Capo, 2011), 70

Zadie Smith, *Changing My Mind: Occasional Essays* (The Penguin Press, 2009), 66

Blake Snyder, *Save the Cat! The Last Book on Screen-*

writing You'll Ever Need (Michael Wiese Productions, 2005), 49

Claude M. Steele, *Whistling Vivaldi* (Norton, 2010), 26

Michael Stocker, *Hear Where We Are: Sound, Ecology, and Sense of Place* (Springer, 2013), 12

Cheryl Strayed, *Wild* (Vintage Books, 2012), 75

T

Henry David Thoreau, *Walden and Civildisobedience* (Penguin Classics, 1983), 39

Eckhart Tolle, *The Power of Now* (New World Library, 1999), 69

Heather Tosteson and **Charles D. Brockett**, editors, *Connected: What Remains As We All Change* (Wising Up Press, 2013), 69

Peter Turchi, *A Muse and a Maze: Writing as Puzzle, Mystery, and Magic* (Trinity University Press, 2014), 46

Lao Tzu, *Tao Te Ching* (Addison Wesley, 2000, reprint edition), 42

W

Janine Wedel, *Unaccountable: How Elite Power Brokers Corrupt Our Finances, Freedom, and Security* (Pegasus, 2014), 8

Terry Tempest Williams, *When Women Were Birds: 54 Variations on Voice* (Picador, 2012), 87

ABOUT THE EDITORS

The members of Team Olsen have long since overcome the feeling that the other was hogging all the creative molecules in the house and exerting undue pressure on noisy keyboards. After four-plus decades of wordmongering, Cheryl and Eric happily maintain separate home offices, literary tastes, and styles. The husband and wife writers edit each other's written work—and sometimes spoken language as well. Every once in awhile, they put aside their respective creative endeavors to work on a project together that renews their faith in the transformative power of words. This book is one of those projects.

www.ingramcontent.com/pod-product-compliance
Lightning Source LLC
Chambersburg PA
CBHW030445300426
44112CB00009B/1172